This book

55
50¢

YOUNG MEN CAN CHANGE THE WORLD

Books by Booton Herndon:

BERGDORF'S ON THE PLAZA

YOUNG MEN CAN CHANGE THE WORLD

young

men

can

change

the

world

BOOTON
HERNDON

McGRAW-HILL BOOK COMPANY, INC.

New York
Toronto
London

65-7071

Though this book mentions by name many individual chapters and many officers and members of the Junior Chamber of Commerce over the world, it would be impossible, of course, to identify them all. It is to those unnamed thousands of chapters, those unnamed millions of good Jaycees who have served so well over the past years, that this book is respectfully dedicated.

CONTENTS

I | *FOR THE BROTHERHOOD OF MAN*

INSIDE A MUD-WALLED HUT in a remote jungle village in Vietnam a young American stood quietly, watching the small group of people clustered around an old door which served as an operation table. On the table lay a native woman, victim of Communist atrocity, emaciated and pitiful. Bending over her were a Filipino doctor and nurse, a Malayan nurses' aide, two Vietnamese assistants.

How many more nationalities were represented by that little group, the American thought. . . . Burmese and Thais and Japanese, French and Germans, Moroccans and Israelites, people from a hundred countries of the world who had sent medical supplies, food and money to the suffering people of this unhappy land.

For this was Operation Brotherhood, the first great program of Junior Chamber International, that unique organization of the young men of the world, the Jaycees. And right here in this native hut, thought David O. Haxton, the twenty-six-year-old secretary-general of JCI, as in other makeshift hospitals all over Vietnam, Operation Brotherhood was proving the truth of the Jaycee belief that the brotherhood of man transcends the sovereignty of nations.

As Haxton watched, the doctor put down his instruments. He turned to the forlorn native squatting in the corner, the patient's husband, and, smiling, indicated that everything was going to be all right. And then, suddenly, the husband was on his knees before the doctor, sobbing with joy, kissing his hands. Tears burst from the eyes of the doctor, even as he tried to pull his hands away. Tears burst from the eyes of the nurses, the assistants, and, finally, even Dave Haxton.

"For I realized," Haxton said later, "that he was not only kissing the hands of the doctor, but the hands of every Jaycee in the world."

How many thousands of lives have been saved, how many millions of suffering persons have found surcease from pain, how many billions of tears have been dried by the activities of these young men? Nobody knows. Yet, incredibly enough, all of their service to mankind, to their own nation, their community, is but a by-product of the primary aim of this American-born organization.

For the express purpose of the Junior Chamber of Commerce is leadership training, to help the members of today become the leaders of tomorrow.

And so its membership is restricted to men between the ages of twenty-one and thirty-five. "Just when you think you know what you're doing," a former national president once said ruefully, "you've got to get out."

The worth of the leadership-training phase of the Jaycee program has been proved over and over by the successful careers of so many of its former members. Its graduates include business and professional men; mayors, governors, Congressmen and Senators; leaders in many of the countries of the world.

Men of influence and power recognize the value of this training. When a group of Los Angeles businessmen, dissatisfied with their representation in Congress, formed the famous Committee of One Hundred to find and back a rival candidate for the office, they named Henry Kearns, one of their number and a former national president of the United States Junior Chamber of Commerce, to the screening committee. This committee met several times, interviewing aspirants.

One day Kearns learned that a young attorney to be interviewed was a Jaycee. Aha, Kearns thought, here's a young man who's been through the best training program in the world. He took over the questioning at that session. The young man made a most favorable impression, first on the screening committee, then on the group as a whole. He became Congressman, then Senator, then Vice-president. His name: Richard M. Nixon.

Even a generation ago government leaders went to the Junior Chamber to find the top leadership in young men. In 1932, President Herbert Hoover summoned Jaycee president George H. Olmsted to the White House and asked him how to interest young men in the Republican Party. Olmsted, then thirty years old, suggested forming Young Republican Clubs throughout the nation, and was promptly given the job.

The Republicans took a shellacking that year, getting only some sixteen million votes, yet in four months Olmsted signed up four million young Republicans—one-fourth of the total number of voters. And twenty years later the Young Republican Clubs played a big role in another landslide, this one in their favor.

And by that time, too, George Olmsted had become one of the great financial leaders of the world, a millionaire many times over, and a major general in the United States Army.

Another evidence of Jaycee leadership is in the American flag itself, for to the United States Junior Chamber must go much of the credit for bringing Alaska, and consequently Hawaii, into the Union.

While these young men are attending their practical college of leadership they seem to take on unique, inspiring characteristics—part dedication, part comradeship, part sheer exuberant energy—that cut through prejudice and stuffiness. In North America there's an all-Chinese-American chapter in New York's Chinatown; an all-Negro chapter in Chicago, an all-Indian chapter in Montana, an all-Eskimo chapter in Alaska, and an all-Dukhobor chapter in Alberta. In many locals, of course, and in the state and national organizations, members of different races and religions all serve together.

It's the same in other countries too. In Asia, where Jaycee chapters form a rim of freedom around the area of Communist domination, erstwhile colonists and colonials work together in Jaycee councils. In Vietnam, for example, there are both French and Vietnamese Jaycees, and there are both English and Malayan Jaycees in Singapore. The board of directors of the Hong Kong Junior Chamber contains an Englishman, a Portuguese, a Chinese, an Indian, and a Malayan.

Perhaps the most amazing proof of JCI's motto, "Young men can change the world," took place in Israel, where Arabs and Jews have been at each others' throats for centuries. There the Tel Aviv chapter invited the sheik of the largest Arab tribe in Israel to be guest speaker at their goodwill luncheon, and made him an honorary member.

The sheik then invited his fellow Jaycees to his desert camp, fed them royally with the traditional Arab dinner, then had his tribesmen put on a dazzling display of horsemanship for their benefit. It was quite a day.

The United States Junior Chamber of Commerce is, of course, a full member and the largest by far of the Junior Chamber International. Each of the states elects a JCI director. One director returned from the World Congress in Tokyo in wide-eyed wonder. He told his fellow Jaycees how the delegate from India made an impassioned plea for the admission of the Pakistan Jaycees, being embraced by the Pakistan Jaycees when he finished, and how France and Belgium together supported the admission of Germany.

But the invocation impressed him most of all. As a Buddhist Jaycee from Hong Kong led the delegates in prayer, the American saw a Moslem Jaycee from Morocco standing between the Jewish Jaycees from Israel and the Christian Jaycees from New Zealand, all with heads bowed in reverence.

Back home, the Jaycees listened to their director's report with interest. He was, incidentally, A. M. "Red" Ghahremani, a red-headed Persian from Watsonville, California.

Many world leaders see in JCI a positive hope for world peace. Vice-president Nixon reported on his return from a trip to Asia that the Junior Chamber was doing more to stem the tide of communism than any other non-governmental organization. The people of Asia could hardly bring themselves to believe what their own eyes saw in Operation Brotherhood, that fantastic international project in which the Jaycees of the world poured men, money, and supplies into Vietnam to aid the refugees from communism.

"Never before in history," breathed the president of the Vietnam Republic, Ngo Dinh Diem, in wonder and awe, "have the people of one country of Asia helped the people of another in this way."

New and sparkling and hopeful as this bright dream of world brotherhood may appear to some, to the young visionary who founded the Junior Chamber almost a half century ago, this was no dream, but a prophecy. For, as Henry Giessenbier, the almost-forgotten genius who founded the Junior Chamber of Commerce, wrote in the early days:

"From within the walls of the soul of this organization, wherein the foundation of character and good citizenship are laid, I hope a message will come in the sometime of tomorrow that will stir the people toward the establishment of a permanent and everlasting world peace."

Projects, Projects, Projects

Every spring, in a Jaycee meeting somewhere in the United States, you can count on an eager young Jaycee standing up and making an impassioned speech about that terrible, grassless, brown spot in the park. When he finishes the president promptly appoints him chairman of a committee to do something about it—namely, plant grass.

So the eager young Jaycee consults the manuals, pesters the director in charge of community development and the vice-president in charge of external programming with a thousand questions, promotes enough grass seed, fertilizer, and agricultural implements to seed a fair-sized county, drives the radio station and newspapers crazy with smudgy releases and excited telephone calls, and, finally, lures a bunch of Jaycees out to the park on Saturday and Sunday and gets the grass in.

Everybody tells him what a wonderful job he's done and he goes home and tells his wife he thinks he'll run for office next year.

Months pass. The excitement of Christmas is in the air. Another eager young member delivers another impassioned speech, this one on the terrible fire hazard comprised by dried-up Christmas trees in homes all over town. Why not collect them all, pile them up and have a big bonfire?

So, ten seconds later, he is chairman of the Christmas-tree-burning committee. He, too, reads all his manuals, promotes enough transportation to haul a national forest, sends out reams of publicity and finally puts on a big bonfire, right in the middle of the park. It's a terrific success—if you live upwind, that is.

Winter ends, spring comes—and there's a great big brown spot, right in the middle of City Park. And so an eager young Jaycee springs to his feet and says that somebody ought to do something about it. And so it goes, year after year.

Projects, projects, projects. . . . A newly organized Junior Chamber in a small Western town once decided to buy the community a disaster truck. Jaycees have contributed hundreds of such vehicles to communities throughout North America. So, they ordered the truck. Bright red, with shiny new equipment, it was a beauty. But how were they going to pay for it? Easy—they'd raffle off a car. A dozen committees were appointed, and they all charged around having tickets printed and getting publicity and organizing teams of salesmen, and sure enough, they sold enough tickets to pay for the vehicle.

Next week somebody remembered they'd never paid for the automobile.

And on at least one occasion a Jaycee project had official Washington all shook up. Even though it was named the Project of the Year at the Buffalo convention, what went on behind the scenes was so hushed up that even the top Jaycees didn't know the real story. But now it can be told:

The Strasburg, Virginia, Chapter dreamed up the excellent idea of planting white pine seedlings in historic soil and presenting them, as Liberty Trees, to famous national personalities, including the President of the United States, the Cabinet, and members of Congress. The soil came from Jamestown, the Alamo, Yorktown, the Shenandoah Valley, Valley Forge, and Bunker Hill.

In that soil lay not only the seedlings of the Liberty Trees, but the seeds of a government explosion. For although the Jaycees had, of course, Department of Agriculture approval for the seedlings, it had never occurred to anyone that the historic soil also had to be officially O.K.'d. After the trees had all been shipped, out of the blue sky came an announcement from an

agriculture official that they would have to be recalled
—there might be bugs in that soil!

Well, Virginia's Representative Burr Harrison,
through whose office the Jaycees had made the presentation, nearly blew his top when he heard the news. He
wrote President Eisenhower a letter, telling him that
his own Department of Agriculture was going to throw
him in the hoosegow if he planted that Liberty Tree.
He was dissuaded from mailing the letter only at the
last minute, when the department decided that, well,
maybe that historic soil wasn't so contaminated after
all.

To a person unfamiliar with the whole idea of the
Jaycee movement, even the big time-honored projects
have their aspects of irony. Take the nationally known
Jaycee-sponsored golf tournaments like the Los Angeles
Open and the Insurance City Open in Hartford. There
you find the Jaycees working long, hard hours while the
golfers make the headlines, win the money.

At the International Ski Tournament at Alta, Utah,
the shivering Jaycees stand in the snow all day long,
guarding the markers as skiers from all over the world
whip down the course. And at night there is no room
at the inn for the weary, frost-bitten Jaycees who
started the whole thing in the first place, for everything
is booked solid by skiers and out-of-state fans, months
in advance.

Or take the Phoenix rodeo, the world's biggest. Before the event Jaycees put all chutes and corrals in A-1
condition. During the event they ride herd on the
orneriest critters alive—not the broncs, but the six
hundred-odd hard-bitten cowboys competing for the

prizes. And after it's all over, well, *somebody* has to clean up after all those horses.

This well-organized rodeo has netted the Phoenix Jaycees as much as $40,000 in one year. What do they do with the money? They give it all away, in one night, to any and all reputable agencies which can show a good reason for asking for it.

To Jaycees, none of this seems at all strange. Every Jaycee project, whether a whopping success or a colossal flub, provides leadership training. "The real purpose of our organization," said Edward A. Merdes, of Alaska, 1959 national vice-president assigned to leadership, "is to develop the leadership capabilities of our members through planning and executing projects which make our communities better places in which to live."

The typical Jaycee, the young man who is going somewhere in the world, finds joy in work, a thrill in accomplishment. David Rohrer, for example, program manager of the national headquarters staff, has been consultant on many of the great national Jaycee projects.

"But I have to confess," he once said, a little wistfully, "that the most fun I ever had in Jaycee work was when I was on the bottom rung of the ladder back home in Pennsylvania. Somebody gave a big old house to the blind of the city, provided the Jaycees would clean it up. A flood had washed tons of silt into the basement and we had to shovel it all out. It was hot and stuffy, and back-breaking work, but we were all working together, doing something for somebody, and we had a few beers down there too, come to think of it, and, well, I remember it as one of the happiest days of my life."

There's a fierce pride and *esprit de corps* in this organization. Jaycees believe they can get more done than anybody else in the world, and leap at any opportunity to prove it.

For years, in Charlottesville, Virginia, at Christmas time, the Jaycees have been manning the Salvation Army fund-raising kettles on one side of Main Street, challenging any and all other organizations to do as well with the kettles of their own on the other side of the street.

"They've been throwing a pretty strong lineup against us lately," Edward H. Deets, Jr., the Charlottesville president said with a grin. "Lions, Kiwanis, Exchange, Falcons, Rotary, even the local reserve unit of the United States Marines. But we still raise more money, year after year, than all the rest do put together. Bring on the Army, Navy and Air Force—we'll still whip 'em!"

Esprit de Corps

In the United States alone, Jaycees number 200,000 young men—average age, thirty; average yearly income, $6,000—in some 3,700 Junior Chambers. Individual chapters vary as widely as do individual members. Most locals welcome any reasonably presentable young man between the ages of twenty-one to thirty-five to membership. At the other extreme are the big city locals—New York, Chicago, Detroit, San Francisco, Los Angeles—which would shudder at the thought of accepting anyone less than a junior executive.

The Los Angeles Junior Chamber, for example, pays its executive secretary twice the national average Jaycee income—$12,000 a year. It doesn't even elect officers, but appoints them. "To analogize to our operation," Robert L. Meyer, 1959 president, explained, in all seriousness, "I would say that a corporate type of organization, rather than a political type procedure, would obtain."

The largest Junior Chamber of all, the 1,400-man Rochester, New York, chapter has an entirely different organizational set-up. It has one central group, seven branches.

Whether wearing a gray flannel suit in an air-conditioned office, or dungarees and blisters in the hot sun, all Jaycees who get anywhere at all in the organization put in plenty of hours of hard work. In addition, those who aspire to higher office must face the travel grind. The national president visits many locals in every state including, of course, Alaska and Hawaii, in addition to representing the organization at important state, national, and international events.

The ten vice-presidents attend all important functions in all states in their assigned territory. Each state president attends all national, regional, and state meetings, as well as visiting the individual chapters. The 246 national directors, one for every twenty-five locals, must visit those locals, as well as state and national meetings. The seven hundred-odd state vice-presidents must visit the chapters in their territory, as well as all state meetings.

From the top down, they all spend far more money

than their travel allotments. And finally, of course, anyone aspiring to the next higher office has to get out and campaign for it.

Death of a Young Man

Why do these young men spend their own time, money, and sweat, day after day? Why do they take off at the end of a working day, appear at a meeting tens or hundreds of miles away, get back home just in time to go to work bleary-eyed, then repeat the whole process again that night? Why do they endanger their finances, their health, their home life? To many people—indeed, to many Jaycees—these sacrifices just don't make sense.

Therefore, for the benefit of the cynics, the scoffers, and the unbelievers, it might be wise at this point to make, and then prove, one simple stark statement about this driving force, this Jaycee movement:

Men have given their lives for it.

There was Harold A. Marks of Phoenix, Arizona. He was scheduled to install a new chamber at Douglas one night, but couldn't get away from the office in time to drive there. He chartered a plane and talked the pilot into flying him to Douglas—even though the pilot had never flown at night before, for this was in 1924. "I'll take the risk," Marks said. The plane crashed and both he and the pilot were killed.

Then there was Clayton Frost, North Carolina Jaycee president, killed in an automobile crash while returning from the installation of a new chapter. And only a few months later, Clint Dunagan, Texas president, died in an airplane crash.

But even though these men gave the ultimate sacrifice, their lives, their heroism cannot compare with that of a serious, intense young man from Gainesville, Florida, Seldon Waldo, president of the United States Junior Chamber of Commerce in 1946–47. Waldo did not merely risk his life for the Junior Chamber, nor did he lose it suddenly and swiftly in a blazing crash.

No, Seldon Waldo paid out his life slowly, deliberately, agonizingly, over a period of months, knowing what he was doing every minute.

Waldo had suffered an acute attack of nephritis when a boy, which left his kidneys in a weakened condition. Doctors told him he could never lead a normal life.

Nor did he. He led a life far more strenuous, far more demanding, than normal. He drove his way through college and law school, was a successful attorney in Gainesville while in his twenties, and became a city judge. All this time he was forging his way up the Jaycee ladder of success—local officer, state officer, national office. Work, travel, shake hands, speak. . . .

And the strange thing was that Waldo was by no means the popular conception of a club man. A little shy, reserved, he did not meet people easily, was not a good speaker. But what he lacked in warmth, personality, and God-given talent for swaying a crowd, he made up for by hard work and self-discipline. Although Waldo never pumped your hand and pounded you on the back, when he shook hands with you his well-trained mind remembered who you were, where you were from, and what you wanted. Although he cast no spell when he gave a speech, that speech was based on painstaking research. It was solid, factual, and concise.

When he was a candidate for the national presidency, he arrived in the convention city, Milwaukee, in a special train filled with Florida beauties and a carload of orange juice, plus copious quantities of additional spirits to add flavor. He even had a professional campaign manager.

Waldo's main campaign issue was the proposal to raise national dues from $1 to $2 per individual member. It met bitter opposition. National dues are not paid directly by members, but by locals out of their treasury, according to membership. It was the big locals which protested the most. The maximum amount per local at the time was $400; under Waldo's proposal it would be doubled to $800.

But Waldo considered the increase essential to the future of the Junior Chamber. That year, 1946, the organization was in a great postwar upsurge of membership. Membership had doubled. But this had placed a great strain on the administrative staff. The executive vice-president and his few assistants had been working nights and weekends attempting to service the organization. There just wasn't enough money to hire more people, install better equipment.

And through lack of funds the Junior Chamber had missed out on some splendid opportunities. It had been invited to send a representative to the United Nations, a delegation to the Peace Conference in Paris, but could not afford to accept either invitation. Presidents and vice-presidents spent thousands of dollars out of their own pockets.

"We are living in crucial times," Waldo told the convention. "Never before have young men been faced with a greater challenge. We want to build an organization which can give you the assistance and help to which you are entitled. We want to make this great body of young men, with its loyalty, its ideas, and devotion to our country, a great force for justice and peace. Working together we can not fail."

It was a rough and tough campaign but Waldo was elected. The dues were raised, and the United States Junior Chamber of Commerce began its great new surge to the position of power and respect it occupies in the nation today.

But the new president found himself in the center of a storm of protest. The big locals were threatening to pull out. What was Waldo going to do? There was only one thing he could do: Appear personally before them, plead, cajole, explain the issues in order to hold them in the national organization.

And so he traveled about the country, from New York and Hartford and Boston to San Francisco and Los Angeles and points in between. He flew in prewar DC-3s, he jounced over wartorn highways, he swayed in old railroad cars over bumpy roadbeds.

Before running for office, Waldo had checked with his personal physician. He had been told that he could stand the rigors of the presidency provided he paced himself, and that Waldo had coldly planned to do. But now it was impossible. After six months of hectic traveling, operating under terrific pressure from the bitter opposition, trying so desperately to hold the Junior Chamber together, Waldo began suffering those familiar, nagging, pains. He went back to his doctor, and the doctor, after a thorough examination, laid it on the line:

Unless he quit traveling immediately, took a long rest, his life would be endangered.

That night, after the children had gone to bed, Waldo discussed the whole thing calmly and dispassionately with his wife, Tommy Ruth. They talked it out for hours. They agreed, together, that it was his duty to continue as president, his duty to preserve the Junior Chamber of Commerce.

"I'd rather give everything I've got to hold the Jaycees together and die because of it," he told Tommy Ruth that night, "than live on knowing I haven't done my best."

And she, knowing Seldon Waldo for what he was, and loving him for it, gave him her blessing to continue.

Neither of them ever mentioned the true state of Waldo's physical condition. Not even Frank Fister, the executive vice-president who traveled with Waldo, who saw his face become gray and lined with pain as the dreadful months went on, knew the real truth.

Waldo finished his year. He held the Junior Chamber together and he increased its programs, stature, and potential.

And then he collapsed. Death was not quick and merciful; it came on leaden feet. He died in 1950, after two years of helplessness and pain. Not until years later, and then only to a few intimate friends, did Tommy Ruth reveal their secret, that death had been Seldon Waldo's own deliberate choice.

Think what you will of the Junior Chamber, this is the way one of its members laid his life on its altar.

2 | *YOUNG MEN CAN BE CHANGED!*

MANY A MAN has spent long hours trying to come up with a good definition of the Junior Chamber of Commerce. Here's one that comes as close as any: Horatio Alger come true, and multiplied ten thousand times.

Thousands of young men have found their wildest ambitions realized through the Junior Chamber. This movement has changed the lives of more young men, and with more dramatic impact, than any other similar organization in the history of mankind. Working in, for, and with the Junior Chamber can, it has been proved, turn a tongue-tied young rube into a poised executive, an assembly-line worker into a multi-millionaire, a so-called egghead into a practical politician. . . .

Such an organization is no more, no less, than the men who have served it, and who have been served by it in return. And so, here are some capsule-sized stories of successful men who give credit to the Junior Chamber for much of their success. . . .

From the large, lush offices of George H. Olmsted, Major General, United States Army Reserve, president of the International Bank of Washington and of the Financial General Corporation, comes the direction of multi-million-dollar enterprises around the world. In

18

the United States alone General Olmsted's corporations own banks with resources valued at over 700 million dollars, five life insurance companies. His overseas interests include consumer-credit operations in Thailand and the registry of the Merchant Marine fleet of Liberia, third largest in the world; over half of the really big tankers are under this registry.

Yet, at one time, George Olmsted had no idea of following a business career. He was an outstanding cadet at the United States Military Academy, top-ranking cadet officer, and second in his class. Not until after a tour of duty did he return to his native Des Moines and enter business there.

"George was brilliant, all right," said one of his hometown friends, Allen Whitfield, national Jaycee president in 1935–36 and an attorney of national prominence. "But it was membership in the Jaycees which smoothed off those sharp military edges and enabled him to be a success in the civilian world."

When Olmsted was summoned to Washington by President Hoover he was apprehensive and nervous all the way across the country to Washington, and thence to the White House. He was only thirty, and in those early days of the Junior Chamber, Jaycee presidents did not always meet national presidents. But he kept telling himself one thing: *In his underwear, the President of the United States looks just as ridiculous as I do.*

On the threshold of the President's study, young Olmsted paused, closed his eyes, pictured the President in his underwear, and then went in. The session went off without a hitch. With success in the United States

Junior Chamber of Commerce and the Young Republican Clubs behind him, Olmsted went on to become a success in international finance.

Here's another success story, that of a young factory production worker named Clifford D. Cooper. Sharp and energetic, an around-the-clock worker, Cooper had worked up to an executive position with his company when he became Jaycee president in 1949. During his term he presided over a great reorganization of the Junior Chamber; afterward he did not return to his company, but, instead, started all over again, with a small machine shop.

For, Cooper figured, if he had learned anything at all, it was organization and administration. And where was this experience most needed? In the new field of guided missiles and rocketry, where, in too many cases, brilliant scientists were attempting to be both technician and administrator.

Cooper was right. He gradually gathered scientists and technicians around him, and his management know-how permitted them to put their time and brains exclusively on what they knew best. And so it was Cooper-built rockets, equipped with Cooper-built electronic instruments of the most sensitive nature, which flew into the mushroom of the first hydrogen bomb. It was Cooper-built instruments in Cooper-built rockets which made the precise measurements of the energy transmitted from sun to earth during the total eclipse of the sun during the First Geophysical Year. It was Cooper-built apparatus which comprised the last three stages of America's first lunar rocket.

Late in 1958, the big Marquardt Aircraft Company

of California traded Cooper 2 million dollars worth of Marquardt stock for an equal number of shares of the Cooper Development Corporation. In four months Marquardt stock doubled in value. And so, in that four months, Cooper netted 2 million dollars without moving a finger.

Many Jaycee presidents have gone on to big things in the business world—like Lee Price, Jr., of Swainsboro, Georgia, former FBI agent and OSS officer, who became vice-president of the Coca-Cola Company just a few years after serving his term of office.

Some young men climb the ladder of financial success right along with the Jaycee ladder. Frank Pasquerilla joined the Johnstown, Pennsylvania, Junior Chamber when he was a young state highway employee. He worked hard, made contacts, proved his ability in both Jaycee activity and on the job and got backers in both fields. And so, at the age of twenty-seven, Pasquerilla was both president of the Johnstown Junior Chamber and president of Crown Construction Company, doing a million dollars' worth of business. By the time he was thirty, he was a national vice-president of the Junior Chamber, and his multi-million-dollar company was handling big jobs all over the east.

Completely at the other end of the pole, about as far from a businessman as you can get, stands Paul D. Bagwell. He is not only an academician, a doctor of philosophy, but a classical rhetorician, a scholar of Aristotelian philosophy. Bagwell, as one of the top ten graduates of the University of Akron, had been awarded a year's membership in the Akron Junior Chamber. After getting his Ph.D. and becoming an assistant instructor at Michigan State University at Lansing, he remembered the Junior Chamber and sought to join the Lansing local. It nearly bowled the members over—he was the only faculty member who'd ever thought of such a thing—but they welcomed him nevertheless.

Although Bagwell had been left badly crippled by polio during his undergraduate days, he didn't let his physical handicaps keep him from getting out and working. He steadily forged ahead up the Jaycee ladder, serving as local, state, and national officer, and in 1948 achieved the young man's dream—president of the U.S. Jaycees.

Even then, although he'd gone through some rugged campaigning, Bagwell's only interest in governmental politics was theoretical, based on Aristotle's ideas of 2,300 years before. But as retiring president of the Junior Chamber, Bagwell was the natural choice to head up the Citizens for Eisenhower movement in Michigan. Thus, when Eisenhower was elected President, Bagwell found himself one of the leaders of the Republican party in Michigan. Believing that through continued participation in politics he could contribute to his community, his state, his nation, and, for that matter, the Republican party, which in Michigan had fallen into the doldrums, Bagwell remained active. In 1956, he ran for auditor general of the state, and although the Republicans were crushed in the Democratic landslide, Paul Bagwell led his party ticket. In 1958, he ran for governor. Again the Republicans lost, but again it was Bagwell who led the ticket. And this time it was much closer.

And so Paul D. Bagwell, Ph.D., became the leader of the Republican party in Michigan. "And I can assure you," he said with a grin, "that if it hadn't been for the Junior Chamber of Commerce, I would never have dreamed of running for anything."

An equally incongruous Jaycee politician was Ted Anderson, the colorful, Bohemian artist and TV consultant of Salt Lake City. One year Anderson, as a prominent Jaycee, took part in the annual Jaycee mock legislature, a well-planned, highly publicized state-wide event. He liked it so much that he ran for the legislature next year, made it, and at the age of twenty-nine was named the outstanding member of the house.

Or take the case of Edwin H. May, Jr., a young businessman of Hartford, Connecticut. May ran for Jaycee national president in 1955, putting on a terrific campaign and leading in the first ballot, only to go down before a coalition. He went back to Hartford with his campaign organization intact. What could he do with it? Well, the Congressional election was coming up. Although the incumbent had won in this predominantly Democratic district by 36,000 votes, May threw his hat in the ring as a Republican. With the organization which had almost, but not quite, won for him the Jaycee national presidency, May was elected to the Congress of the United States by a plurality of 22,000, a switch of 58,000 votes.

One day a young man was ambling down the street of the old river town of Owensboro, Kentucky, wondering what he was going to do with himself now that he was out of the Army. He strolled in a store to look at electric razors. The store owner, showing him the latest

models, asked if he belonged to the Junior Chamber.
He left the store with a $20 razor and an invitation to
join the Jaycees.

Nine years later, in 1956, that young man, Wendell
Ford, was national president of the Junior Chamber.
He took an interest in Junior Chamber International,
and remained active in JCI. He traveled the world
over, conversed with leaders of many lands. And the
young man from Owensboro became a man noted for
his international aplomb and suavity.

Sometimes the Junior Chamber has made it possible
for a young man to fulfill the secret dreams of boyhood.
Marvin B. Koonce, as a boy, dreamed of travel, of far-
off places. But his dreams were at conflict with his ambitions, which were to serve his family's public storage
interests, and be a successful businessman and respected citizen in his home town of Raleigh, North
Carolina. How could a man have both?

As Marvin worked his way up the Jaycee ladder to
state president, to national treasurer, he also took an
active interest in Junior Chamber International. The
JCI spirit nurtured his boyhood dreams. He attended
four World Congresses, in Mexico City, Edinburgh,
Tokyo and Minneapolis. He became an active member
of the JCI economic affairs committee. He served the
cause of JCI abroad, and he brought its message home
to North Carolina and all the states.

And when Marvin set out for his fifth World Congress, in Rio de Janeiro in 1959, he did not go alone,
but as one of a group of North Carolina businessmen
on a special mission from the governor. They visited
several European countries, acquainting industry with

the advantages North Carolina could offer. Then Marvin proceeded on to Rio, to serve the cause of international understanding, and finally returned to his community and business interests with a sizable increase in experience and stature. Where else can a man eat his cake and have it, too?

One of the Junior Chamber's most inspiring stories is that of Tom Marshall of Jackson, Mississippi. When Tom was just a boy his mother died, his father became ill, and on the bitterest day any child could possibly imagine, he found himself in a public institution, a lonely, frightened, embittered boy, just six years old.

Tom ran away again and again, only to be caught and receive cruel beatings. Then he thought of another way of getting out of the institution. He worked hard in school, made a good record, and, when he was fourteen—he looked older—got a night job outside the home. Thus he put himself through high school and business school, learning accounting. He was twenty years old, a bookkeeper at the local power company, when a friend came to him with an urgent request. The friend, a Jaycee, had just been presented with a pregnant rabbit. He had to take care of that rabbit and her unborn progeny until he found a new member for the Jackson Jaycees. Would Tom please, please, sign up?

"Frankly," Tom Marshall said later, "I was scared to join. I wanted to, but I was afraid that, with my background, I'd do or say the wrong thing, and be ridiculed. But I screwed up my courage and joined. I'd been in only a couple of months when a local photographer took a picture of a couple of us sticking some Scotch-

Lite on an automobile bumper, and it was published in the paper. I couldn't get over it—there was my picture in the paper! That one little thing gave me more of a sense of security than I could have gotten in years."

Tall, handsome, with a pleasing personality and a quiet but driving ambition, Tom worked his way up the ladder. His company noticed his development, took him out from behind the pencil, put him into public relations. At the national convention in Buffalo in 1959, Tom was reminiscing with a friend. "In my last year at the orphanage," he was saying, "there were six guys who ran around together. Today two of them are in the state penitentiary, two in the federal penitentiary and another is a fugitive from justice. And the sixth, that's me, is running for the national presidency of the United States Junior Chamber of Commerce."

Sometimes it's easier being a poor boy than a rich boy. Take the case of Jim Cashman, of Las Vegas, Nevada. Jim's father was the first settler in Las Vegas, did well, and Jim grew up in his shadow. Wherever Jim went, the old-timers said, "Boy, you'll never be half the man your father was." Jim heard it so much he almost came to believe it. And he rebelled. Maybe he couldn't make as much money as his father did, maybe he couldn't discover great new frontiers—but, by God, he could drink more whisky and raise more hell!

He drifted into the Las Vegas Junior Chamber, but at the time it was only a luncheon club, and he rarely attended. Then, one day, one of the fellows called him. A group had chartered a plane to go to Chicago for the national convention, but one of them had canceled out. Would he like to go? Jim went along, just for the ride. But at the convention something strange and marvelous happened.

For at this convention Jim Cashman saw men no older, no smarter, no stronger, no wiser than he himself, accomplishing things in their own right. He heard them make bold, yet carefully thought-out proposals, listened to them deliberate, make thoughtful decisions which would affect their lives and the lives of thousands of others. He saw the fury and intensity of the election in which leaders of this dynamic group were selected.

And suddenly, there on the convention floor, Jim realized that the last frontier had *not* been conquered, after all. It was right here, a frontier of young men, and it would go on and on, repeating itself year after year after year.

Jim was moved, tremendously, by that convention. When, on the plane going home, he blurted out this new-found emotion, he found that some of the other fellows felt just the same way he did. Enthusiasm swept the plane. They would build up their own Junior Chamber, make it as good as any other.

"If those other guys can go out and get blisters on their hands," Jim Cashman cried out in the plane, "we can too!"

And so Jim Cashman found a frontier right where his father had found it, right there in Las Vegas. He and the other ambitious young men got together, brought in more men who thought the way they did, outvoted the do-nothings who thought the Junior

Chamber was a luncheon club, and took over the whole chapter. Before long they were doing things, too, just like the other Junior Chambers over the nation. Jim became state president, chairman of a national committee, and then he ran for national vice-president.

Of course, there was no possibility of his making it. Not only was he from the smallest state, population-wise, in the union, with the smallest number of supporting votes to start out with, but in many circles, Jim knew, he was considered a playboy. All along, he had steadfastly refused to be a hypocrite. He flew his own plane, spent money when he wanted to. But he loved this organization, he had given it all he had, and had made thousands of friends. That would have to be enough.

And it was. Jim Cashman, plane, bankroll and all, was the first and only national vice-president ever elected from Nevada.

Incidentally, while Jim was working his way to the top of the national Jaycee movement, he was taking over more and more responsibility in the business at home. He quietly made changes, getting rid of some lines, taking on others. One day his father retired, happy and secure in the knowledge that he was leaving his business in good hands.

"You know," Jim once said, a little incredulously, "I honestly think my father's proud of me."

The Junior Chamber has taken many a hesitant young man and made a positive go-getter of him. It has changed introverts into extroverts. Many people know that Bernard B. Burford, hail fellow professional secretary-treasurer of Optimists International, used to be Illinois state Jaycee president—but how many know that he was a research chemist before that?

"Sometimes I remember that quiet little laboratory I used to be buried in," Burford said, "and I ask myself, 'what the hell am I doing here?' "

But the Junior Chamber has softened young men in the right places, too. John Holgate, of Phoenix, hard-driving, personally ambitious, could say, even when he was twenty-five, that even his ulcers had ulcers. John was handing out toys at the annual Phoenix Christmas party, a huge affair at which thousands of underprivileged children are regally entertained, then give thousands of dollars worth of presents, when he noticed that a little Mexican boy to whom he handed a cap pistol was not wearing shoes.

John pulled the little boy out of line and asked him where his shoes were. The boy was scared and flustered. His mother saw the confusion and, thinking the boy had misbehaved in some way, hurried over, contrite and frightened. John asked her where the boy's shoes were. She began crying, and said her child had none. John looked down at the boy with a cap pistol but no shoes, looked at the crying mother. "Let's go," he said gruffly. He took mother and boy by the hand, led them to a store, and bought the child a pair of shoes. As the boy walked up and down in the store, trying out his new shoes, still clutching the presents he'd brought from the party, looking ten feet tall, the mother confessed, sobbing, that this was the first time her child had ever received a present of any kind.

"Then why are you crying?" asked John Holgate.

"Because I'm so happy, *señor*," she answered.

And, suddenly John Holgate felt something warm coursing down his own cheeks. He too was crying, crying tears of joy in the realization that it is indeed more blessed to give than to receive.

To some people, Jaycee activity has even meant a smaller income—and that's the way they would have it! Take the case of Carlos Fernandez, born in America but raised in Cuba, who arrived in Miami almost penniless. He put himself through law school with money he earned tutoring Spanish. Quick and sharp, Carlos saw right away that he could build a lucrative practice among fellow Latin Americans. He was well on the way to being a very wealthy young attorney when he joined the Junior Chamber. At first he was just another member, until he went to his first convention. Although he went only to have a good time, he came back home imbued with the Jaycee spirit. He threw himself into Jaycee work. Even though he knew some prejudice against Cubans existed in Miami, he dared to run for president. He gave the campaign all he had, and he was elected president by an overwhelming majority.

"I'm a better man today because of the Junior Chamber of Commerce," he said frankly, "and I'm grateful. I used to spend all my spare time drinking, gambling, and chasing women. Through the Junior Chamber, I've found that nothing can be more rewarding and actually enjoyable than working for your community and your fellow man. I used to feel like a foreigner, but through membership in the Junior Chamber I feel like a member of America, too. I could make a lot more money if I restricted my practice exclusively to Latin Americans. Only I'll be damned if I will. I'm an

American now and I'm going to have an all-American practice."

For every Jaycee leader who has made a million dollars, or achieved national fame in political or business circles, there are thousands more back home who have still gone farther than they ever dreamed, thanks to their Jaycee activities. The reason is simple: The Junior Chamber, throughout the world, gives its members an opportunity for leadership. Take the case of Evan L. Hultman, of Waterloo, Iowa. Hultman joined the army when he was eighteen years old, during World War II. He was platoon sergeant at nineteen, company commander at twenty, battalion commander, with the rank of major, at twenty-one. After the war, he was president of the student body at Iowa University, district attorney of Waterloo, and candidate for state attorney general.

"But," Hultman said, "I got more leadership training in the Junior Chamber than in all my other activities put together. I hadn't been in the organization eight months when they appointed me chairman of the annual band jubilee. They gave me $5,000 and told me to arrange a complete program for seventy-eight bands from seventy-eight different communities. My military experience was great, sure, but this was training for civilian activity, for living in the world as we know it. Where else can a young man get such an opportunity to learn?"

The Man Who Made His Dream Come True

It seems almost eerie, but the man who founded the Junior Chamber of Commerce believed, years before his contemporaries did, that just such an opportunity

to learn was not only possible, but that he, Henry
Giessenbier, could create it. Henry Giessenbier, known
to his friends as "Hy," was a man who lived far ahead
of his time. Like many another prophet, his vision and
work were recognized and appreciated far more by the
generations who followed him than by his contemporaries.

"To understand the enormity of what Hy Giessenbier dared to dream," Andrew H. Mungenast, his life-
long friend, explained, "you've got to put yourself in
St. Louis back in, say, 1915. St. Louis was an old town,
a conservative town, a dead town. Most kids quit school
when they were fourteen and went to work. You can
imagine how long it took a young man without even
a high school education to learn to be a competent
executive, to make a prompt decision, to address a
group. Why, a man would be in his forties, at least, before he had the experience and background to accept
responsibility, either civic or corporate. Young men
just simply didn't stand a chance."

Most young men accepted this. Not Hy Giessenbier.
(The name is pronounced *Geese*-n-beer, incidentally,
and means "to pour beer" in German.) Hy, too, son of
a German-born waiter, had to quit school in the eighth
grade. But he didn't let that stop his education. He
read voraciously, and he thought about what he read.
Thomas Jefferson, he read, wrote the Declaration of
Independence when only thirty-three years of age;
twelve of its signers were also under thirty-five. But,
Hy observed as he looked around him, a young man in
St. Louis didn't even stand a chance of being a minor
clerk before he was thirty-five.

Something should be done to change this way of thinking, but what? Well, one way would be to organize. Although young Giessenbier himself was not so much an organizer as a creative dreamer, there was, after all, nobody else to do the job. And so Hy took the dancing clubs, as the young people's fraternities were known in those days, and forged the bigger and better ones into one federation. Henry was president; Andy Mungenast, secretary-treasurer.

About this time, in 1915, a group of civic-minded men started thinking of ways to improve the run-down part of town. Construction of a parkway would help. They organized a speaker's bureau. One of the best speakers was a former Shakespearian actor named Huse N. Morgan, who had lost an arm and retired from the stage. The old-timer, now known as Colonel Morgan, delivered a particularly moving address. In the audience was Henry Giessenbier. After the meeting the young dreamer approached the old thespian and volunteered the support of the young men of the community. The colonel snapped him up immediately.

Using the federation as a nucleus, Henry sent out a call for more young men. And so, on the night of October 13, 1915, thirty-two young men met in the attic room of the Mission Inn, on the corner of Grand and Magnolia Avenues. Hy's father was headwaiter at the Inn and he got the room for nothing. Enthusiasm swept the small room, and they agreed unanimously to form an organization. They chose the name "Young Men's Progressive Civic Association." Giessenbier was elected president and Andy Mungenast secretary.

How many similar clubs have been founded, only to

die of apathy and lack of leadership? But Giessenbier put this organization on the right track from the very beginning. Civic betterment was the goal of the association, and this meant action. Not discussion, *action*. Enthusiasm spread.

This was what the young men of St. Louis, without knowing it, had been looking for! Within six months the YMPCA had a membership of 750.

There was plenty of work for them to do. The Democratic national convention was held in St. Louis in June, 1916. The young men got out and scrubbed the town in preparation for it.

This was the forerunner of every clean-up, fix-up, paint-up campaign in the world.

Then Clarence H. Howard, millionaire president of a big steel company and president of the Business Men's League of St. Louis, stepped in. Howard took over the Young Men's Progressive Civic Association like a mother hen. He gave the group money out of his own pocket, promoted for them an old art museum as their headquarters. Talk about your white elephants— the building hadn't been painted for years, and its ceilings were thirty feet high. But the young men promoted paint and brushes, rigged scaffoldings, and painted the whole thing themselves.

The old museum became a beehive. There were study groups in salesmanship, banking, accounting and public speaking. Membership was over 1,000. Still Howard hovered over the organization. He saw it as a kind of continuation of the Boy Scouts. He prevailed upon the YMPCA to change its name to Junior Citizens.

When World War I came young Giessenbier, patriot and zealot, organized the Junior Citizens into a full company: Company L of the Missouri Fifth Infantry. He even found a company commander: Dwight L. Davis, later to become Secretary of War, and the donor of the Davis Cup tennis trophy.

And what was the president's rank in this company? He went into World War I a buck private and came out a buck private. But he served gallantly. A friend of his reported later how Hy was crawling grimly forward in the Battle of the Argonne, bullets whining over his head, shells bursting all around.

Another soldier dived into a shellhole, called out, "Come on in here, that fire's too hot." But Giessenbier kept crawling forward, grimly, toward the enemy. A second later another shell burst right in the middle of that shellhole. A helmet flew out. Giessenbier's refusal to dog it had saved his life.

Members of Company L came home after the war to find the organization still going strong. John H. Armbruster, the beloved third member of the early triumvirate of Giessenbier, Mungenast, and Armbruster, had helped keep it going.

But there had been one big change. The Business Men's League of St. Louis had become the St. Louis Chamber of Commerce. Immediately Daddy Howard, still its president, had wanted the Junior Citizens to change their name again. Out of this came a new name: The Junior Chamber of Commerce.

And ever since, although many Jaycees have cordially hated the word "Junior," and others have maintained that the organization has nothing in common with any

Chamber of Commerce, senior or otherwise, the name has remained. Not for many years, as a matter of fact, did the word "Jaycee" come into approved usage. Nor could a local Junior Chamber be called a chapter, club, local, or anything but just that: Junior Chamber.

During the war, young men in other cities had heard of the success of the St. Louis Junior Citizens, and somewhat similar groups were being organized elsewhere. Now Giessenbier dreamed of making the Junior Chamber a national organization. He sent out letters to other cities, calling an organizational caucus. Representatives of twenty-nine cities appeared.

In his keynote speech, Giessenbier set forth at length his proposal for a national organization of young men. "My fellow delegates," he concluded, "may I say that in your hands lies the destiny of a great organization. Let us build it to national recognition. Let us organize in it the interest of young men for a greater America. Let us not fail in this task."

The first convention was held June 17–19, 1920, in St. Louis. Henry Giessenbier was elected the first president of the new national organization.

He worked like a horse that first year. He wrote hundreds of letters. He worked all night, many a night, on organizational details, turning his dreams into plans, plans into reality. And all this time he held down an important position; at the age of twenty-six he had become cashier of a local bank, the youngest bank officer by far in St. Louis.

During that first year, a young man from Tulsa named E. Fred Johnson came through St. Louis. Johnson, too, was a restless young man with a driving ambition. Only twenty-four, he had already become well known in Tulsa, and was one of the founders of an organization of young men known as the Secotym Club. Giessenbier took him to lunch, tried to interest him in the National Junior Chamber. Johnson wasn't really interested, but Giessenbier sized him up just right. When Johnson got back to Tulsa, he found a letter officially appointing him to the nominating committee for the second annual convention to be held in Dallas. Johnson could hardly refuse, and, once he had accepted, he was morally bound to go to Dallas.

At the convention Johnson found that the other members of the nominating committee had drawn up a slate of officers headed by the incumbent and founder, Henry Giessenbier. Johnson had nothing against Hy, but he felt that a man should not succeed himself. Purely as a matter of principle, he drew up his own slate of officers and presented it as a minority report. His presidential candidate was George O. Wilson of Dallas, handsome, a forceful speaker, and a hometown boy. He picked the rest of his slate on a geographic basis. Johnson was probably the most startled man at the convention when the Johnson slate was elected in toto.

And Henry Giessenbier, who had founded the organization, who had poured his soul and energies into it, suddenly found himself without portfolio.

Thus was born the tradition that no national president can succeed himself. This policy, broadened out to the point that *no* officer can succeed himself, has worked extremely well, of course, in relationship to the avowed purpose of the Junior Chamber, which is leadership training. For it throws every office open all over again each year.

The defeat of Giessenbier, however, had a more direct bearing on the Junior Chamber in the early twenties. George Wilson, and his three successors— Raymond T. Wilber of Springfield, Massachusetts; Harry B. Mortimer of Milwaukee, Wisconsin; and Lou Arland of San Diego, California—were all competent, personable men, but they did not have the almost religious fervor that the St. Louis founders had.

In the meantime, E. Fred Johnson had largely lost interest in the Junior Chamber. Then the Mayo Hotel was built, and Tulsa set about looking for conventions to fill it. Johnson was prevailed upon to go to the 1924 convention in order to land the 1925 convention for Tulsa. He did, and wound up getting elected president at it.

Johnson, a talented organizer and executive who finished what he started—he went on to organize and become president of one of Tulsa's largest banks—put the Junior Chamber back on its feet. He established a good magazine, which served as a bond between members, served as personal ramrod for an expansion program, and got the organization on a sound business basis.

During the years Hy Giessenbier, who had founded an organization for which he had dreams of greatness only to helplessly watch it stagnate, unquestionably had moments of sadness. It seemed as if he were forgotten by his own creation. Fortunately, he was rising high in banking circles during those years. Many of his depositors insisted upon entrusting him completely with the investment of their funds.

But the Junior Chamber had not forgotten Henry Giessenbier. It could do little for the founder when he was riding the wave of prosperity, but it could help him when tragedy struck. And tragedy did strike. When the stock market crashed, the depositors for whom he made investments lost money. Although fortunes were lost all over the nation, these people tried to blame it all on Henry Giessenbier. They brought charges against him.

And it nearly crushed this sensitive man. Henry Giessenbier, founder of one of the world's great movements to aid mankind, would be the last man on earth to cheat one person out of one cent. Here was a man whose integrity shone like a star. And when that integrity was questioned it nearly killed him. He had a complete nervous breakdown. It was his good friends in the Junior Chamber, Andy Mungenast, John Armbruster, Harry Krusz, a younger St. Louisian destined to be of great service to the national organization, and all the rest, who brought money and groceries to the Giessenbier home to keep the family going.

Gradually Giessenbier came out of it. He determined to conduct his own defense. This would mean going through mounds of records at the bank, ferreting out endless streams of figures to justify his activities. One morning he dragged his emaciated form from his bed, dressed, and tottered out to the sidewalk. He stood at the corner, waiting for a streetcar. Suddenly he began trembling, so hard that he could no longer stand up. He had to sit down on the curb.

"I knew then," he told Andy Mungenast later, "that this was my moment of decision. If I gave up then I was through."

He didn't give up. He pulled himself to his feet, got on the car, and rode to the bank. Many months later he stood trial. Using his own figures, he conducted his own defense. He was completely absolved of guilt and the judge gave vent to a caustic criticism of those who had brought the suit in the first place.

Not long after, Giessenbier suddenly became ill and died within a few hours.

What did he die of? "I think," Andy Mungenast said sadly, "that it was a broken heart."

Today Henry Giessenbier's grave is a shrine. It is visited daily by at least one delegation of Jaycees from some part of the globe, near or far. Many visiting Jaycees, particularly the old-timers, ask John Armbruster or Andy Mungenast to go with them. The St. Louis Jaycees have marked an avenue to the tomb with flags of all the nations in the Junior Chamber International. Henry Giessenbier is not forgotten.

And the organization he created out of dreams and plans and hours on hours of dedicated labor is strong and solid. His beloved Junior Chamber now rings the earth.

3 | *THE POSTMASTER GOT A RAISE*

COMING DOWN the long gradual hill from the Tulsa business district, past the new, gleaming office buildings, you can see, across the rich green expanse of Boulder Park, the long, handsome glass-walled building blending into the far hillside. This is the $750,000 War Memorial building, national headquarters of the U.S. Junior Chamber of Commerce.

The Memorial looks serene and dignified as you approach, but these looks are indeed deceiving. For this handsome edifice is actually the home of controlled confusion, compounded and condensed. Ideas ricochet off the inside walls of this building like cosmic rays. Here a professional staff of a score of trained, creative young men, plus some thirty general employees, try sometimes to lead, sometimes to keep up with, the activities of 200,000 American Jaycees.

Somebody is always coming, somebody always going. A member of the sports staff, just back from snowbound Maine, bumps into the national president, just back from his visitation to the Hawaiian Islands. And two staff members nod good-by; one is going to the tip of Florida; one to the tip of Alaska. The feeling of urgency is catching. After an hour in this atmosphere the new staff member seems to take on an air of haste and purpose even when heading for the lunch room at coffee-break time.

Yet out of this seeming chaos comes order. From the little office of Charles R. Stiver comes the copy necessary to fill the compact, well-written little magazine *Future* each month. From the same office historian Tom Campbell has compiled what is probably the most complete history of any similar organization in existence, hundreds of thousands of easy-to-read words from the very first utterances of Henry Giessenbier down to the exact amount spent on the most recent improvements on the building.

On the shelves of the orderly stockroom are thousands of pamphlets, brochures, project kits. From this room goes forth everything from the voluminous bulk material necessary to stage the Safe Driving Road-e-o on down to the single small postcard reminding tardy locals that dues are due. Literally tons of materials go out of this headquarters each year. When the Jaycees moved to Tulsa, so much more mail flowed through the post office that the postmaster got an automatic raise.

All of this leads to the oft-asked question: Why did the Jaycees come to Tulsa in the first place? The answer is complex. For one reason, an Oklahoma delegate to a national convention once made a joking remark. For another, the delegates to a state convention lost a little money in an all-night poker game. But perhaps it would be best to begin at the beginning. . . .

For years the U.S. Junior Chamber of Commerce had no permanent headquarters. Even after it had an official executive secretary, the dedicated Harry Krusz of St. Louis, one of the early leaders of the organization, headquarters still was where the president lived. After each election, Harry packed his bags and moved to a new city. It was rough on Krusz, but his continuing faithfulness to the Junior Chamber over the years certainly helped the young organization through some trying periods.

In 1934, the Chamber of Commerce of the United States offered the Jaycees a permanent headquarters in its building in Washington, D.C. For years the Junior Chamber had been wondering whether it really was a Junior Chamber of Commerce, and here was an opportunity to decide, once and for all. And so, at the fall, 1935, meeting of the board of directors it was officially decided that the Junior Chamber was completely autonomous. Since then the two organizations have maintained a friendly relationship but not an official one.

After declining, with thanks, the free offer of space in Washington, the Junior Chamber headquarters were set up in the founding city, St. Louis. Four years later headquarters were moved to Chicago, as *Future* magazine was then being published there. Dougals Timmerman, the live-wire executive vice-president of 1942, made arrangements with the LaSalle Hotel to take over the twentieth floor for Jaycee offices. This floor had formerly housed the hotel laundry and the ceilings were low. Thus Timmerman got it cheap. For several years Jaycees could be spotted easily; they walked stooped over and had lumps on their heads.

During the war years, Tom Baldridge, a long-active, colorful Virginian who has added much to Jaycee history, proposed a War Memorial to the Jaycees who had given their lives to their country in World War II. As so frequently occurs in Jaycee matters, the man who produced the ball was permitted to run with it, and Baldridge did. Entirely on his own he traveled the country over, making speeches at Jaycee meetings and conventions, seeking contributions. He raised thousands on thousands of dollars in war bonds. Gradually the form of the War Memorial took shape in the minds of Baldridge and his committee as a permanent national headquarters.

At the 1944 convention in Omaha, Baldridge took the floor and called for war bonds for the Memorial. State after state pledged bonds. Charles Kothe, Oklahoma state president, sprang to his feet and cried, "Oklahoma pledges its share of the bond quota." Then, on the spur of the moment, he added—"and invites the U.S. Jaycees to make their headquarters in the youth capital of the world, Tulsa, Oklahoma!"

Kothe's words not only stunned the convention but the Oklahoma delegation as well. It was the boys from Oklahoma City who recovered first. What right, they wanted to know, had Kothe, as state president, to invite the Jaycees to his own home town? Anybody with half a brain knew that Oklahoma City was the garden spot of Oklahoma, not Tulsa.

And so the battle raged in Oklahoma for almost a year, until the next convention. Then it developed that Tulsa and Oklahoma City were deadlocked for state support. They might still be deadlocked had it not been for a poker game. The Enid delegation lost their shirts to the Oklahoma City delegation. Next morning, bleary-eyed but determined, the Enid delegation cast its vote for Tulsa.

Of such things is history made.

Of course, this meant only that Tulsa had the state's approval to bid for the honor. Several other cities presented bids, but now a young Tulsa Jaycee, Dick Gode, was determined to bring headquarters to Tulsa. Gode raised a guarantee of $100,000, and promoted the promise of free office space until the headquarters building was built. He carried the bid to the meeting of the executive committee at which the final decision would be made.

And there he came down with a serious hand infection. It was swollen, inflamed, and agonizing. He kept having more penicillin pumped into it. Flushed, almost delirious with a high fever, he should have been in a hospital, but he refused to leave. He made his speech of invitation, listened to the others, heard the committee award headquarters to Tulsa, and then collapsed.

Baldridge's committee raised $150,000, and so, with Tulsa's $100,000, it had a quarter of a million dollars to build the War Memorial. A contest was set up, with several industrial sponsors and an outstanding panel of judges, and a prize of $10,000 to the architect submitting the winning design. Unfortunately the prize-winning design had to be modified—the low bid was for $150,000 more than the Jaycees had.

The building was completed in 1951, and equipped with $15,000 worth of modern furniture. Four years later the first floor was extended. In 1959 a third floor was added. These improvements brought the worth of the entire property to a current value of at least $750,000.

This building, incidentally, is not owned by the Jaycees. It is owned by a separate organization, the Jaycee War Memorial Fund, which rents it to the national organization for a fixed, nominal fee. There's a good reason for this; the fund is a non-profit organization, and as such, not subject to taxation. Tom Baldridge is chairman of the fund. Baldridge was also honored for his contribution to the Jaycees by being made an honorary member.

Within the $750,000 building, the U.S. Junior Chamber operates on a $600,000 budget. The financial mainstay is the $2.50 per capita income from its 200,000-odd members. Use of mailing lists brings in about $50,000 a year. Few people realize it, but tucked away in the basement of the building is a mail-order business doing $250,000 gross a year. This is the Jaycee supply section, which sells everything from a little booklet, "Welcome to the Jaycees," at four cents a copy in lots of one hundred, to a highway sign for $35. But the main business is done in lapel buttons. Jaycees buy 75,000 of all kinds a year, for a total of $40,000.

"Jaycees are good customers," Dick Simpson, the manager of the supply section, says with a grin, "we turn over our inventory four or five times a year, and we never have a bad account."

Bankers and businessmen who are unfamiliar with the Jaycees simply can not comprehend the fact that responsibility for this budget lies in a group of young men who change office every year. Every March the 300-odd members of the board of directors come into Tulsa to approve, or disapprove, the recommendations of the finance committee and the executive board. The board meeting begins at 8 A.M. on a Friday. Usually the president, as a matter of interest, asks how many have ever been in Tulsa before. About 25 or 30 of the 300 raise their hands. Yet by Saturday night, they will have poured over a monumental financial statement, okayed —or kayoed!—the expenditure of money for hundreds of separate items like $50 for equipment repair in the mailing department, $142,701 for publication of *Future.*

The board is no more a rubber stamp organization than is the Congress of the United States. Indeed the organization is based, roughly, on the same principle. Each of the fifty-one Jaycee states is represented regardless of population, as in the United States Senate, and is also represented on a population basis, as in the House of Representatives. The 300-man board of directors is composed of the state presidents, the national directors, who are elected at state conventions according to state membership, and the executive committee. The executive committee is composed of the president, immediate past president, ten national vice-presidents, the executive vice-president, treasurer, general legal counsel, vice-president for North America of the Junior Chamber International, Canadian president and Mexican president.

This governmental system was set up after many hours of study by a committee under the chairmanship of Kenelm L. Shirk, of Lancaster, Pennsylvania. The Jaycees could hardly have picked a better chairman, for Shirk had been an eager-beaver Jaycee since he was nineteen years old. At the time he was going to law school in Carlisle, fifty miles away. He hitchhiked each way, and, when stranded in a town between rides, would hunt up young men and tell them about the Junior Chamber. Thus Shirk helped organize other Junior Chambers before he was a bona fide member himself. At one time, before Shirk was thirty, he was legal counsel for U.S. Jaycees, Junior Chamber International and the Pennsylvania Jaycees all at the same time, as well as holding state office.

And while on the subject of young men looking for work, take Walter Weller of New Jersey, 1958–59 treasurer. It had long been customary for the treasurer to take the previous year's budget, make it fit the current year's demands. The recession of 1958, however, had eaten into the 1958–59 income. Rather than save a few pennies here, shave a little off there, Weller threw out the whole budget, and started all over again from scratch. It took him long hours, night after night after night, over a period of months. Nor was it a welcome relief from his job, for Weller, as treasurer of a large pharmaceutical house, saw more than enough figures during the day.

One of the items not even Walt Weller could pare is travel expense. Everybody travels, and of course it is the national president who travels most of all.

The Jaycee president's finances are an open book. He lives rent free, with all utilities paid, in a $75,000 home. Living allowance for the year is $6,000, moving allowance $1,000. Travel allowance is $9,500, which must take him some 250,000 miles throughout the United States, Alaska, and Hawaii. He also attends the World Congress of the Junior Chamber International, whether it be Minneapolis in 1958, Rio de Janeiro in 1959, or Paris in 1960.

It's practically impossible for a Jaycee president to get through the year without spending several thousand dollars more than he is alloted. Nor is he finished then.

"Nobody told me, when I was running for office," genial Charles E. Shearer, Jr., said with a wry grin, "that the year after I was out of office I'd still be running around like a chicken with its head cut off. A past president is lucky if he can spend half of the days of the month at home. He's a member of the executive committee and must attend all official national functions. He's on the board of Junior Chamber International, and must attend its more important functions. He's on the board of directors of the U.S. Chamber of Commerce and I also happen to be active in the Young Republican Club. In addition, the Jaycee past president is in great demand as a speaker. It would be selfish of him to refuse all requests. I make several a month. And all he has to do with the rest of his time is make enough money to pay back what it cost him to be in office in the first place!"

For the few days and nights that the president can spend with his wife and children, at least he has a lovely home, the Jaycee White House, to come home to. Like so many things in the Jaycee world, the White House came about through an impulse.

It was when Dain J. Domich of California was president that Mike Maloney, then president of the Arkansas Jaycees, drove to Tulsa to bring the national president to Arkansas for a regional conference. He stopped off

at the beautiful War Memorial headquarters, then proceeded to the president's house. And he found the
president, his wife and five children, crowded into a
dreary frame residence, miles across town from headquarters. Rent $175 per month, plus utilities.

Mike was appalled. Was this the way the Jaycee president should live? Back home in Arkansas he set out to
do something about it. He went to one of the largest
lumber yards in the state, exacted a promise to furnish,
free of cost, all the lumber for a Jaycee White House.
He went to a furniture manufacturer, promoted a
complete houseful of furniture if and when there was
a house to put it in. With this as a starter, he interested
other states. Then at the Colorado Springs convention
in 1954, he took the floor to propose that each state
chip in and build the Jaycee White House. It was en-
thusiastically adopted, each state promising to contribute, and Mike Maloney's dream was on the way to
reality.

As in the case of the War Memorial building, a contest was held, and the prize-winning design proved too
costly. Modifications were worked out, and construction began. Into the house went the very finest of materials, the very latest of conveniences, all gifts of Jaycees from coast to coast. Some of the gifts are priceless,
such as the irreplaceable china presented by the New
Jersey Jaycees. Others are most practical, such as the
annual fire insurance policy presented by the Connecticut Jaycees. Jim Cashman flew a group of Nevada
Jaycees in with an automatic sprinkling system, which
they installed themselves. And a particularly nice fea-
ture is that each outgoing president takes with him all

the linens his family has used—rich, lush towels, fine percale sheets and pillowcases, presented each year by the North Carolina Jaycees.

It takes the new president and his family just about one minute to move into their plush new home. When Bob Clark, 1959–60 president and his wife arrived in Tulsa, for example, they found that the Tulsa Jaycees had the house all spic and span, and dinner in the stove. Then the local members moved in the new family's belongings, and washed the dinner dishes. When it came time to retire, the beds were all freshly turned down.

It was just like coming home.

4 | *HOW TO MAKE*
A HALFBACK CRY

WHAT WOULD YOU GIVE to be president of the United States Junior Chamber of Commerce? $100,000? Your business? Your profession? Your life? Four years of business seniority?

Those are only some of the prices Jaycee presidents have paid over the years. It was not even a national president, as a matter of fact, but John Shaffer, a former president of the New York State Jaycees and a much-sought-after trial attorney, who figured he lost $100,000 in referred cases which he could not handle.

Several Jaycees—Henry Kearns and Horace "Hunk" Henderson, to name two national presidents—gave up lucrative businesses for Jaycee activity. Chuck Shearer gave up his law practice to become president of the Jaycees. It was Seldon Waldo who gave his life. Hugh McKenna, executive with Mutual of Omaha, points out that to be president requires two years of hard politicking, one year of actual service, and another year of limited activity—a total of four years during which time the young company executive simply can not devote full time to his work.

"And during those years," McKenna adds wryly, "the other fellows in the company were not standing still."

But the rewards of the presidency are great. No other young men in America, not even movie stars, are so lionized as the Jaycee president during his one year of office. He must visit every state at least once, and every state, every local he visits rolls out the red carpet of welcome for him. He's a judge at the Miss America contest in Atlantic City, a featured guest at the Phoenix Rodeo, a VIP at the Apple Blossom Festival in Virginia, to name just a few events he attends with bells on. He is also, of course, the star at every state and regional convention and conference he can attend, not to mention the convention at which he wins his honor, and the convention at which he presides.

If the Jaycee movement as a whole is a great college of practical experience as many have described it, the intensive experience gained by the one top leader of the movement must be a valuable post-graduate course indeed. The national president hobnobs with senators, governors, congressmen, and, frequently, the President of the United States. He goes from Jaycette teas to cocktail parties to banquets to stags, making speeches as he goes.

But though the president is wined and dined, though his year gives him experience and entrees, it is still quite probable that the main reason the Jaycee president strives for that goal is just to prove he can win it. What a challenge! Although it's true that one of the 200,000 members of the Jaycees will be president, the odds are far more than 200,000 to 1.

First of all, he must ascend to the throne by means of steps which, although there have been exceptions, have become stereotyped through the years. The man elected

Jaycee president these days will most probably have been president of his local Junior Chamber, state vice-president, national director, state president, and national vice-president, in that order. Further, he must get to the top step before his thirty-fourth year. Thus, a Jaycee from a big city with a burgeoning Junior Chamber, such as Los Angeles, San Francisco, or New York, where it takes a man ten years to get to be president of his local, would have little hope of gaining the national presidency. On the other hand, if he started out too young, went ahead too fast, he might conceivably wind up on the next-to-last step while still in his twenties, and be considered too young to run.

And if he is from a small state, he starts with just that many fewer votes than a candidate from a large state. The odds against a Jaycee from Washington, D.C., ever making the presidency are much more than 200,000 to 1.

Though the Jaycee conventions are filled with fun and frolic, though prominent speakers talk seriously on important subjects, though weighty decisions influencing the future of the organization are made, the fact remains that the main business at any Jaycee convention is to elect a slate of officers, particularly a president. To the thousands of delegates and their wives, this is tremendously exciting. The intensity and emotion mount up over hours and days, until you feel you just can't stand it. It's like sitting through the most thrilling football game ever played for three full days, with marvelous entertainment between the halves.

When the election gets under way, nothing else matters. At the 1951 convention in Miami Beach, the featured speaker for the banquet, Senator Richard M. Nixon, arrived shortly before the scheduled hour of eight o'clock. Shrimp cocktails were set at every place, several thousand in all. Waiters stood ready—but nobody came to dinner! The delegates would not leave their balloting, not even for a temporary adjournment to eat and hear Senator Nixon. It was after midnight before they adjourned, but by that time the caterer had ordered the shrimp cocktails thrown into the garbage. Nixon, fortunately, had grimly stayed on.

At the 1954 convention in Colorado Springs, plans were made to adjourn at seven, then repair to the inaugural banquet. A ranch-style caterer had come all the way from Texas with huge trailers and kitchens, and had set up his operations in a circus tent. At the stroke of seven chefs began putting five thousand filets on the charcoal grills.

But the delegates refused to adjourn. E. Lamar Buckner, of Utah, was leading the other two candidates, W. L. "Jack" Howard of Louisiana and James Kirk Newell, Jr., of Massachusetts, but neither of them would give in. Howard and Newell figured that the delegates might turn from Buckner in desperation born of hunger pangs. As the night wore on these hunger pangs caused the delegates to be more irascible and suspicious. And so one state delegation would challenge another, with the result that every man in the delegation from the challenged state would have to parade before the credentials committee and be physically checked off. In at least one case, the challenge proved to be well founded; one man had donned an orange jacket and paraded past the committee with the other orange-jacketed Jaycees of Florida. He almost got away with it too.

At ten o'clock the big ball was supposed to begin at the Antlers Hotel. Set ups were ready, waiters standing at attention, ready for the mob to come in at ten. They didn't know that back at the stadium chefs were still nursing charred lumps of filet.

In the stadium, it began to get cold. The wind came blasting down from the snows of Pikes Peak. Delegates began burning papers to keep warm. Still the balloting continued. And finally at four o'clock in the morning, the sky growing light in the east, a shivering Buckner was elected president of the freezing Jaycees. The inauguration ceremony was held then and there, on a rough, wooden platform under bare electric light bulbs.

In 1959, at the exciting, hugely successful Buffalo convention, careful steps were being taken to insure that *somebody* would be inaugurated at the inaugural banquet, whether the new president would make it or not. It's a good thing such arrangements were made, because when the noisy Jaycees finally did elect their new president, the inaugural banquet was long gone.

On the first ballot, big Ed Merdes of Alaska got off to a flying start. Behind him came Bob Clark of Iowa, Ed Selleck of New York, Tom Marshall of Mississippi, and Milton Taff of Alabama.

Merdes was far short of the majority required, however, and so another ballot was taken. The situation wasn't changed. In the third ballot, Selleck, the popular, crew-cut New Yorker, with his pretty wife Nancy on his arm, withdrew from the race. Another ballot, re-plete with ear-splitting demonstrations, was also inconclusive, and Milt and Eloise Taff went to the rostrum and, as the crowd cheered his valiant effort, bowed gracefully out of the race.

After the next round the presiding office declared an adjournment for the inauguration banquet even though there was still no president to inaugurate.

But there were ten good men and true who had been officially elected and could thus be inaugurated—the national vice-presidents. The big crowd at the National Guard Armory in Buffalo cheered them all as they were introduced. There were the usual cries of "Stand up, Bucky!" as Uriel "Bucky" Blount, Jr., the short-in-stature, but long-in-wit, Floridian, already on his feet, grinned at the old joke. They cheered Jeff Davis of Georgia, TV and motion picture executive who, at the age of twenty-nine, had already traveled more than most men travel in their entire lifetime. Then came Morgan J. Doughton, the solid, dependable Pennsylvanian, and Dr. Robert Easton, the go-getter dentist under whose leadership Maine Jaycees established a record number of new chapters.

Byford Elwonger, the hard-working and experienced Nebraskan who was also JCI Senator No. 1760 and who brought the state of Nebraska 100 per cent into the JCI fold, was next. And then came A. M. "Red" Ghahremani, Persia's red-headed gift to California and the Jaycees.

Charles Rodermel, as former school teacher, principal and current education supervisor for the Wyoming Game and Fish Commission, was a natural for the Youth and Sports portfolio. He was followed by Tom Ruffin, Louisiana businessman already honored with the Seldon Waldo award as national chairman of the extension committee. After the businessman came the farmer, F. John Taylor of Illinois, whose accomplishments in community service and farm organizations made him a natural for the Community Development portfolio.

And, finally, last in the alphabet but certainly not last in force and drive, was Howard J. Thomas, Maryland attorney who also won a Clayton Frost award as an outstanding state president.

Hardly had the cheers quieted for the ten vice-presidents when it was time to go back to balloting for the top position. Five times the ballot was taken, and five times it was revealed that no candidate had the majority. And then, handsome Tom Marshall, his sorrowful wife Lynn beside him, conceded. Midway during the eleventh ballot, Ed Merdes took the platform, and in a thunderous ovation asked for a unanimous vote for the Jaycees' new president, Bob Clark of Iowa. It was 1:15 A.M.

The Kansas City convention of 1956 was even more memorable, due entirely to the emotion-packed drama which went on there. Mike Maloney, an intense Brooklyn Irishman who had worked his way up to the top of the ladder through his adopted state of Arkansas, and Wendell H. Ford, a personable, soft-voiced Kentuckian, were the front runners with Bob Cook of Illinois and Jack Barnes of Virginia the dark horses.

Jack Barnes, who was admired by many for daring to break precedent and make the race from the office of state president instead of national vice-president, was the first to concede defeat. He did so, in a voice breaking with emotion and in words which made many a delegate wonder if he wasn't the right man, after all.

Bob Cook of Illinois was next to concede. A man of great personal popularity, Cook, too, stirred the delegates with his rousing speech. More hours went by, and the balloting continued. Cook's state of Illinois could not decide on the candidates, and invited both of them to address their caucus. Ford appeared, exhausted, his eyes sunk in their sockets, and spoke quietly for just a couple of minutes on what a fine person Bob Cook of Illinois was, and how he hated to see Bob leave the race. But Maloney, though limp as a rag a moment before he began to talk, somehow found the stamina and enthusiasm to reiterate his policies and promises.

Only after that, learning what Ford had done, did Maloney realize for the first time that he might lose. Only then, although a devoutly religious person, did he pray. But he did not pray for victory. Instead, he closed his eyes, bowed his head, and whispered, hoarsely, aloud, "Oh, God, if I lose, give me the strength to take it like a man."

Illinois was the deciding state. Its vote would tell the tale. *And Illinois went for Ford.* Instantly Maloney was on his feet, crying for the floor. And then, into the already supercharged atmosphere of the convention, he poured forth his soul in a ringing speech of congratulation and the promise of undying support for the new Jaycee president, Wendell Ford. No one, not Mike, not Wendell, not the presiding officer nor the executive vice-president, remembers a word he said. Yet many a Jaycee today will tell you that the greatest burst of oratory, the most moving flow of words he ever heard in his life, came from the lips of Mike Maloney in Kansas City that night.

Although this election was settled in one great dramatic moment, this moment actually climaxed months of arduous campaigning. Would you like the complete, blow-by-blow account of how a man gets to be president of the United States Junior Chamber of Commerce?

Here's how Robert V. Cox, of Chapel Hill, North Carolina, made the grade.

Even as a child, Bob Cox was a person of determination. He came from a long line of aggressive people; his father, grandfather and great-grandfather all died of strokes. As a boy, Bob had a terrific temper. He was a leader, but he didn't really have a great many friends. He was too confident, too cocky, too ready to fight.

Naturally, for his wartime service, Bob chose the Marines. He went through officer's training at the University of North Carolina. He played football there for three years, as a 195-pound halfback. He scored the winning touchdown against Tennessee. And when he finished his playing days, he stayed on as coach.

In his third year of coaching, Bob received a routine invitation to join the Jaycees, and did so. He went to a couple of meetings, wasn't too serious about it. His first Jaycee job was at the very bottom rung of the ladder. He had to get two hundred dollars' worth of ads for the Carolina directory. He didn't know that this was the worst job of the year. He just went ahead and did it.

His next job was Youth Fitness chairman. He staged

a golf tournament and other events, all successful. Traveling to a district meeting one night a friend of his, Solly Phillips, said to him: "Bob, you're going to be national president someday." Bob laughed.

Not until he was president of the Chapel Hill Junior Chamber did Bob really begin to realize what the Jaycee movement was doing to him. He was no longer the cocky, aggressive young battler, always spoiling for a fight. Instead, he looked back at that impulsive young man he had once been, and realized that there had been an emptiness in him. Now, he knew, that emptiness was being filled. He had been blessed by God with a fine physique, the quality of leadership, and an abundance of brains and determination—but never before had he used them for the benefit of others. Now he was aware of the joy of serving mankind.

"When I was chairman of the annual Cerebral Palsy drive," Bob mused one day, "I went to the home where those afflicted children lived. I saw them walking around with their braces on, all of them wearing football helmets to keep them from hurting themselves when they fall down. They are always falling, always hurting themselves, and yet they are always getting up, always smiling, all of them actually happy, making the best of life despite their handicap. My heart went out to those kids. And I did a better job with the drive, thanks to what I learned from those kids that day. All at once I realized I wasn't so cocky anymore. And I honestly felt I was a better person because of it."

Bob filled in the unexpired term of a state vice-president, was elected national director, then ran for state president. He was elected by a greater majority

than ever before in the state. He stood up before the
shouting people in the big auditorium, his wife at his
side, groping for words. Finally he said, voice breaking, "This is my wife, Cathy," and when the crowd
roared in affection and sympathy, he felt the tears of
happiness begin streaming down his cheeks.

As state president, Bob drove all over the state, being
away from home night after night, every weekend, over
and over. Cathy objected to it at first, but then she went
with him to a couple of regional conferences. She saw
that he was working, working hard. From then on she
was with him completely. If this was what he wanted to
do, and was willing to work so hard for it, she'd be with
him all the way.

After his year as state president, Bob ran for national
vice-president. There were fifteen candidates for the
ten jobs; he figured that delegates would not vote for
ten so much as they would vote against five. He did his
best not to give anyone any reason to vote against him,
and he got the second highest number of votes.

Bob did not immediately announce his candidacy for
president. Some of his friends started talking with
other people throughout the state, sounding them out.
The concensus was that they wanted to back him for
the highest office. Then they put it up to Bob. He
pointed out, candidly, that he had a financial problem.
By now he had left coaching and was partner in a
clothing store in Chapel Hill. He was by no means
financially able to make the race on his own.

His supporters got together, discussed it all over
again, then reported back to Bob. They were with him
to the end. They raffled off a Cadillac, raised funds in

other ways, convinced some North Carolina industries
that the new Carolina watchword, "Make Bob Cox the
National President," was worthy of their support. They
raised thousands of dollars.

A presidential candidate is restricted to an expenditure of $1,500 at the national convention, but he can
spend any amount of money he wants to in his own area.
Bob had the states of North Carolina, South Carolina,
Tennessee, New York, and New Jersey. He was lucky
to have New York and New Jersey. They are not only
populous states, but an entry into New England states
as well.

Bob campaigned heavily in the Northeast and the
South. He did not waste his time on Virginia and
Pennsylvania. Wally Heatwole of Virginia was also a
candidate, and he had those two states.

Bob spared no expense solidifying support in his
own five states. Incidentally, this money is spent only
in travel, long distance calls, mailings, and the like. A
candidate can't actually buy votes. But even so, legitimate campaigning soaks up money like a sponge. Bob
ran out of money during the state convention, and it
drove him crazy. People kept telling him to relax, and
he kept telling them that he couldn't relax with no
money. Finally, his friends took the floor, raised $3,200
for him in thirty minutes, and he was happy again.

The convention was scheduled for June. Bob didn't
stick his head in the door of his business after April.
Now he knew who the rest of his rivals were—Wally
Heatwole, a Jaycee powerhouse from Virginia; Clar-
ence Blasier, a formidable candidate from Ohio; and
Dixie Lynch, a personable, friendly guy from Mis-

souri. Bob had hoped to get the Southern states, as well as ring the coastline. Although a Southerner himself, he followed the moderate policy of his own state in the integration question. Therefore, he arranged for Doc Moses, prominent past president of the South Carolina Jaycees, to make the nominating speech at the convention. Then Clarence Blasier got Bob Silver, president of the Florida Jaycees, to place *his* name in nomination. And Bob lost Florida, right then and there.

Following his coastline theories on the West Coast, Bob got Larry Woodworth, a candidate from Washington the previous year, to help him with the Northwest states. He arranged for the president of the San Francisco local, Vic Levit, to second his nomination at the convention.

Bob also worked on the containment theory. Dixie Lynch, for example, was assigned to the states of Missouri, Iowa, North Dakota, South Dakota, and Minnesota. It was important, therefore, for Bob to get Arkansas and Oklahoma, thus keep Lynch from spreading into Texas.

Another of his ideas was to assign a North Carolina local to each state delegation at the convention. He had to sell the locals on the idea, get them to send their best men, brief them, and, of course, since California is all the way across the country from North Carolina, arrange to get delegations from fifty North Carolina towns out there.

Matching a Carolina local with a state delegation had to be done carefully, too. It would be silly to assign the boys from a rural Carolina town, say, to the delegation from a sophisticated state like New York. Thus locals from the larger cities like Charlotte and Raleigh, were assigned to the largest states. Bob's own local, Chapel Hill, was assigned to California. He was worried about California.

The Cox Campaign Committee chartered two airplanes for the advance party to Los Angeles, buses for the main body. The plane Bob himself was on developed engine trouble and couldn't get off the ground. Bob stayed up all night fretting, until another plane was found. That was the first sleepless night.

State delegations were to be scattered throughout the various hotels in Los Angeles. This geographical distribution was going to cause trouble, as a candidate must address the caucus of each state, squeezing in fifty-one different appearances in three days on top of all other activities. Bob arranged with the Los Angeles local to have a fleet of cars available for him. The drivers of the cars spent several hours exploring all routes between all hotels, determining the fastest route at any given hour of day.

Arrangements were also made to have hot coffee and fresh sandwiches on hand at all times for the candidate, so that he could eat in the automobile between hotels.

The procurement committee obtained walkie-talkie radio sets, so that the boys from the Carolina locals assigned to the state delegations could radio the very latest news into Bob's central campaign headquarters.

Complete dossiers had been prepared on each state, containing such items of information as the state's political traditions, whether individual members like to

drink and raise hell or attend to business. Also prepared were campaign banners for each state—"Arizona
goes for Cox!," for example.

Incidentally, although the banners must be available
immediately, they must also be kept under lock and
key. For they must appear miraculously, as though
from heaven itself. You could certainly never admit to
a caucus that you already had their banners prepared.

And so the convention opened. Bob's transportation
committees, food committee, walkie-talkie delegations
all worked smoothly. He was able to get to several
caucuses that day. Not so much a joke teller and glad
hander as a forceful, dynamic personality, Bob stood up
straight before the caucuses and laid his campaign platform on the line.

Late that evening, a half dozen Arizona Jaycees in
their colorful Western garb walked into Cox campaign
headquarters. They were straight-faced and matter-of-
fact. They made small talk for several minutes.

Finally the leader grinned. "It might interest you to
know," he said, "that Arizona has decided to go for
Cox!"

Bedlam broke out in the room. Drinks were hoisted,
backs were slapped and a crew of Tarheels lit out
lickety-split for the room where the Arizona banners
were hidden. Through the hotel halls and lobby they
went, down to the street, marching, chanting, "Arizona
goes for Cox!"

Shortly after that California came into the fold. More
banners and another parade.

But the next day, though Cox and his cohorts exhorted, used all their wiles, no state made any announcement.

Tuesday afternoon Bob came back to his room to put on a clean shirt. He was going through four and five a day. He ripped off the hotel laundry band, hastily got into the shirt. Then he let out a holler. The thing hung on him like a tent. He could stick four fingers between his neck and the collar. The laundry had sent back the wrong shirt! The campaign committee all began running around feverishly, looking for the candidate's shirts.

Somebody just happened to look in the neckband. There was Bob's laundry mark. It was Bob's shirt. He had lost so much weight that his clothes were already beginning to hang on him.

Just as a matter of curiosity, Bob weighed himself. He was down to 170—he'd played football at 195. And it was only Tuesday—two more days to go.

And on they went. Ground rules prohibit state caucus meetings after 3 A.M., before 7 A.M. However, those four hours were taken up by end-of-day strategy discussions.

Finally it came time for balloting. At the end of the first ballot Cox had 1,178, Blasier had about 500, Heatwole 400, Lynch 300. To anyone not conversant with Jaycee politics that looked pretty good. But Bob knew better. Many a time the front runner at the beginning of the balloting winds up a pitiful last after several hours of election hysteria.

In the meantime the three rival candidates had gotten together and agreed that if they held firm they might knock Cox out of contention. Then they'd battle it out among themselves. And so the balloting went on, on and on and on. And the vote totals varied hardly at all.

Bob and his campaign committee were trying desperately to think up some way to break the deadlock.

Somebody came up with a great suggestion: Vermont! There was only one delegate from Vermont at the convention, and he had two votes. A committee charged out to find this lone Vermonter and sway him to their will. They found him, all right, but they couldn't get close to him. Heatwole had him surrounded like the hole in a doughnut.

Rumors began flying around. A whisper campaign was started among the Georgia and Florida delegations that Cox was a rabid integrationist. It was whispered to the Pennsylvania delegation, on the other hand, that he was a violent white supremacist.

Another ballot, and another, and another. Bob had decided at the outset that he would not do any politicking on the convention floor, lest it be thought that he had pushed the panic button. And so, he sat, calmly, a big, wide, confident grin cemented on his face. But any time a state voted for Cox, and there were dozens of states voting for him on each of the fourteen ballots, the North Carolina delegation arose in a body, beat on drums, hooped, hollered, and led a demonstration, as though this were the very first time.

Another ballot. Things were getting desperate. There was no sign of either of the three giving in. Bob toyed with the idea of challenging some of the state delegations. This would require each individual member to stand before the microphone and state his personal choice. Although Indiana, for example, went for Blazier as a state, Bob knew that he had exactly twenty-six adherents in that delegation, personal acquaintances whom he could call by name.

But if he challenged Indiana, he knew, Heatwole, who had some adherents in California, might turn the tables. And so he decided to leave Indiana alone. Suppose, on the other hand, the Heatwole supporters within the California delegation took it on themselves to challenge their own state delegation? Don't think it has not been done. But the California delegation had prepared for that line of attack. Their biggest, strongest, and burliest men were stationed at the microphones, with instructions to let no one near the mikes except the state president and past president. A Heatwole man would have been torn limb from limb before he could get out a word.

And on it went. Balloting got underway for the fifteenth time. And then, midway in the fifteenth balloting, the entire delegation of the state of Iowa decided that this stupidity had gone far enough. They went to Heatwole, to Blazier, to Lynch, and laid it on the line: If somebody didn't give in, they were going to break the whole thing wide open.

The stalwart three capitulated. They went to the platform, moved that Bob Cox of North Carolina be elected unanimously to the United States Junior Chamber of Commerce. Pandemonium broke out. The motion was carried with a roar. The cry went up for Cox, Cox, Cox. Bob strode to the speaker's platform, erect, holding his head high, trying to keep from crying. As he mounted the stairs, people patting him, shouting words of congratulations in his ear, he was holding his mouth so tight that it became white around the edges, and he overheard someone whisper: "Oh, oh, there goes Bob again."

By the time he had reached the microphone the tears were streaming down his face. No longer could he keep his lips compressed. And so, Bob Cox, ex-tough guy, broke down and bawled like a baby as he accepted the highest honor that can come to a young man, the presidency of the United States Junior Chamber of Commerce.

5 | *JUNIOR CHAMBERS— JUNIOR CHAMPS*

THE PRESS CORPS and gallery following the golfers at the 1958 Jaycee Junior Golf Championship tournament at Columbus, Ohio, were particularly interested in one contestant. The kid was looking for trouble, and everybody was hoping he'd find it. The boy, a skinny youth with long pants turned up over his shoes, would throw his clubs on the slightest provocation. He sneered at his fellow players, talked back to the tournament directors. Other players reported that he was loud and noisy in the dormitory at night, deliberately annoying his competitors.

It all came to a head on the seventeenth hole. The green is like an irregular washboard, impossible to read. The kid took four puts, then heaved his clubs into the crowd.

That did it. The rules committee had just about decided to eliminate the boy anyway. But Jerry Brennan, the Jaycee tournament director (later executive secretary of the Wheaties Sports Federation), insisted on talking with the boy first. After all, such drastic action would have to be reported to the United States Golf Association, which might end the boy's entire golfing career.

Jerry took the boy aside and told him the rules committee wasn't happy with his actions.

The kid sneered. "Well, are you going to throw me out?"

Jerry studied him carefully. Why did he have this chip on his shoulder? After all, he had come over a thousand miles, from a North Plains state, to be in this tournament. The boy knew that his family and friends at home, the local Jaycees who had sent him to the tournament, were following his progress daily in the newspapers. Being eliminated would make a lot of people unhappy.

Although he had plenty to do out on the course, Jerry quietly began trying to gain the boy's confidence, find out just what was wrong. Several things came out. Though the boy had won his state tournament, he came from a state that's dry and flat; golf isn't popular there. The boy had never played on anything but sand greens —no wonder he was having trouble with grass!

Jerry sized up his equipment. Dirty white canvas bag, handful of rusty clubs, old, battered balls. The boy wasn't even dressed like a golfer. Even as Jerry was giving him the once-over, the boy muttered something about his shoes hurting him, and slipped them off. They were Navy surplus street shoes, scuffed and torn, with slick leather soles. Jerry asked him where his golf shoes were.

The boy, surprised, nodded to the battered things he'd just removed. And now Jerry shook his head incredulously. Those shoes brought everything into focus. Here was this poor kid, hopelessly outclassed, with the shoddiest of equipment, trying to get secure footing on strange grass greens with these old shoes! No wonder the boy was trying to make everybody else miserable—he was miserable himself.

And now the boy had shed enough of that phony attitude to indicate that he might be a pretty good kid, after all. He was practically in tears.

Jerry excused himself, hunted up the golf pro, and bought a good-looking pair of golf shoes and three pairs of the loudest socks ever made. He quietly presented them to the boy—and then the tears did come. The boy went out and played a much better game of golf. More important, he wound up as one of the most popular boys at the tournament.

The list of winners and runners-up in the Jaycee golf tournaments over the years reads like a golfing Who's Who. Al Mengert, Gene Littler, Bud Holscher, Eddie Merrins, Doug Sanders, Jack Nicklaus. . . . Yet, despite the great popularity and prestige of the tournament in the golfing world, the Jaycees feel that its unseen, unpublicized features, like making a better man out of a miserable boy through understanding and a pair of shoes, are just as important as the tournament itself.

Jaycees also stage the nation's most important Junior Tennis Tournament. For years Jerry Brennan marveled at the tennis artistry of a perennial contestant, a kid from St. Louis named Butch. "Pound for pound," said Jack Kramer, the all-time great, at one of the Jaycee tournaments, "this kid's the best tennis player in the United States."

But the kid had temperament too. He'd slam his racket into the net, go completely to pieces and miss shots he should have made. In the 1956 tournament at

River Forest, Illinois, Jerry, after watching the boy blow his semi-finals match, had a long conversation with the boy. It all added up to one theme:

"How can you control that little white ball if you can't control yourself?"

After that the two corresponded regularly. In the winter of 1958, Jerry received a typical letter from his young friend. It said, in part, "I'll never forget the lesson you taught me that day in River Forest." The letter was postmarked Australia, where Earl "Butch" Buchholz was playing with the United States Davis Cup team.

The entire Jaycees Youth Fitness program grew out of the dedication and sacrifice of one man, Ray Rice, of East St. Louis, Illinois. When Ray wound up nine years in professional baseball he came back home, went to work as a scout for the St. Louis Cardinals, and organized the Jaycee baseball league. Bob Turley, the $500,000 pitcher for the New York Yankees, was just one of his players.

His local program was so successful that Ray wanted to make it available to boys all over the United States. Naturally he wanted to work through the Junior Chamber.

But that was in 1945. The Junior Chamber had no money for old programs, much less new ones. And so Ray *quit his job, cashed in all of his life's savings, and mortgaged his home for $4,000.* He left his wife and three children at home, and moved to Chicago, where Jaycee headquarters were then. He set about organizing his program on a national basis with his own money, at the same time trying to find financial sponsorship.

Several deals fell through at the last minute, after Ray had spent weeks putting them together.

At the end of the year, all of his savings and mortgage money gone, broke, in debt, and with nothing to show for it, Ray had to go back home, get a job and go to work. A month later a long-distance call came in from Chicago. One of his last contacts, the Athletic Institute, had put up $12,500 a year, plus office space and secretary, for the Jaycee program.

"It's your baby, Ray. When can you come up and take over?"

"I'll catch the next train!" Ray answered. The Jaycee sports program was in business. When Ray left, three years later, to return to business, the program was thriving. His personal and financial sacrifices had paid off in benefits to boys and girls all over America.

Golf and tennis tournaments are but a portion of the work done by the Junior Chamber. Many Jaycees feel that the whole broad program of Youth Fitness is far more important to mankind and the nation.

In 1957, the nation suddenly became aware of what many Jaycees had known all along: American kids just simply weren't getting enough exercise. It was the Reverend Bob Richards, the Olympic champion pole vaulter and one of the Ten Outstanding Young Men of 1956, who got the ball rolling. In Russia Richards had found huge sports facilities, gyms, swimming pools, basketball courts, track and field areas, open not just during school months, but *all the year round*.

"I think it is pretty well proven," Richards said, "that youngsters in Europe generally are more physically fit than our kids over here. *We are soft!* We have kids who can't even do sit-ups and chin-ups. It's fantastic!"

The President of the United States appointed a Council of Youth Fitness. The magazine *Sports Illustrated* went into the project wholeheartedly. The Wheaties Sports Federation underwrote much of the cost. And it was the Junior Chamber, of course, which set out to do the work. It was the Junior Chamber which furnished the name for the project, too—*Junior Champ!*

After all, this was old hat to the Junior Chamber. The Jaycees in San Jose, California, had been doing the job on a local basis since 1931. They had taken a city school fiesta, expanded it into a county-wide program called, fitting enough, Junior Olympics. The big thing was that there was something for even the smallest kid in the smallest rural school to participate in—the 200 kids in the marble-shooting tournament were participating just as much as the uniformed baseball teams of the big schools. And 600 kids won ribbons.

And so when the Jaycees accepted the challenge of the President's Council on Youth Fitness to improve our youths' mental and physical health, they had the know-how and the drive, and did the job right.

The Minneapolis Junior Chamber, always capable and solid, put on the Junior Champ pilot program. It was a year-round project, of course, with the climax coming on Junior Champ Day. There were demonstrations and inspirational talks by some of the greatest athletes in the world, but the real stars were the kids, hundreds on hundreds of them. They ran, they jumped. They rode bikes and worked out on trampolines. And they took a battery of physical fitness tests, including pull-ups, sit-ups, push-ups, jumps, and running events. And those lucky Minneapolis kids proved themselves to be in great shape.

More important, they proved that such a program could be carried on for the benefit and betterment of kids all over the nation. And so today the bustling sports department of the U.S. Junior Chamber of Commerce not only stages world-famous tournaments, but furnishes blueprints and inspiration for Junior Champ programs through the land.

The broad program of national headquarters, incidentally, with all its folders, kits, detailed instructions, and professional personnel, does not supplant or interfere with the projects carried on by state and local Jaycees. Some local projects even augment the national programs. In St. Louis, for example, where Earl Buchholz learned to play under the tutelage of his father, the Junior Tennis program was so popular that the adults wanted in, too. The St. Louis Jaycees accommodated them. They even arranged for cut-rate instruction and 600 adults signed up with Earl Buchholz, Sr., at $10 a year.

For sheer magnitude of operation, the Pittsburgh Jaycees win all the prizes. The Scaife Foundation, with money to spend for youth welfare in Pittsburgh, needed only an organization to administer the program. Naturally, the Jaycees were elected, and found themselves with $50,000. Only proviso: They had to spend it all in one year!

The Pittsburgh Recreation Education Program, or PREP, required much preliminary thought and or-

ganization. At first the Jaycees, as usual, did most of
the work, from administration and public relations to
tacking up signs. But by the time the program reached
the half-year mark it was so complex that a full-time
professional director was hired. And the Pittsburgh
Sun-Telegraph assigned a full-time reporter to it.

The first year, 1958, was a whopping success. The
biggest phase of the program at the beginning was
swimming instruction. Over 86,000 kids participated,
with at least 5,000 completing the primary instruction
and learning to swim.

Over 750 kids took part in the driver-training program. Enthusiasm was high, and results were good.
One of the six winners of the driving contest passed up
a vacation to continue his driving lessons.

Interest in track and field events was low among
Pittsburgh kids, especially girls. But when the Jaycees
got through over 1,200 kids had taken part in track and
field in the first year.

By the end of that year the Pittsburgh Jaycees could
well afford to pat themselves on the back. They had,
indeed, passed the acid test. They had not only spent
the $50,000, but spent it so wisely that the foundation
doubled the amount! The Jaycees began their second
year with the PREP program in July, 1959, with
$100,000 to spend.

Alameda, California, Jaycees also put on a big program—the Junior Olympics. The Jaycees began the
program with grade school kids in hopes that in later
years the Alameda high school track team might win
some meets for a change. Actually the program has
grown far beyond that. Within a few years the Jaycee

locals at Albany, El Cerrito, Castro Valley, Berkeley, and Hayward were participating too.

Incidentally, the Alameda high school track team is now winning its share of meets.

From Bucking Broncos to Rattlesnakes

Why do schools let out for four days in Phoenix in May? Because the rodeo's in town, that's why, and the teachers, like everybody else in Phoenix, learned long, long ago that you can't beat it so you might as well join in the fun.

The Phoenix Jaycee World Championship Rodeo, staged entirely by the Jaycees in March each year, is the biggest and most famous rodeo in the world. From the opening parade—forty bands, fifty floats, at least 2,000 horses, and many riding groups—until the final event four days later, it's impossible for anybody to get any work done in Phoenix, much less the kids. The entertainment—trick riders, square dancing contests, old-time vigilantes—spills right out into the city streets, and the whole town goes Western with a bang.

To the contestants, however, hard-bitten cowboys who follow the rodeo circuit, this is serious business. The Jaycee Rodeo is the gathering place for rodeo talent scouts from everywhere from Madison Square Garden to the Calgary Stampede. Make a good showing at Phoenix and you're set for the season.

Each year over 500 cowboys compete in a dozen different events. Putting on the rodeo requires 100 broncs, 50 roping horses, 20 wild horses, 20 parade horses, 75 bulls, 45 dogging steers, and 100 calves.

But the big story lies behind the chute gates. The

Jaycees have staged their rodeo annually since 1931. It's a year-round proposition. For five weekends before the event, you'll find anywhere from 50 to 100 Jaycees out at the State Fair grounds, putting up fences and chutes. During the four days proper, they sell programs, and, nastiest job of all, try to keep the cowboys in line.

But the work produces results. The Jaycees net as much as $40,000 a year from the rodeo. Nor are all the rewards financial. Part of the movie *Bus Stop* was filmed at the Phoenix rodeo. And for the benefit of cameras the star of the film, Marilyn Monroe, threw her arms around Jaycee president Ralph Feffer, Jr. Wow!

The Phoenix Rodeo is one of some hundreds of tournaments, contests, and athletic events of one kind or another staged by local Junior Chambers from coast to coast. Many of these are major competitions at which world or national champions are determined. Others provide an opportunity for the local talent to develop, and fun for the people of the community.

Just as the Phoenix Rodeo is tops on the professional circuit, so is the Colorado Springs National Intercollegiate Rodeo, also staged by Jaycees, tops in the college circuit. And there's the annual chuck wagon feast that goes with it, too. The whole thing nets the Colorado Jaycees some $16,000 a year.

At the other end of the scale is the rodeo put on by the Madison, Wisconsin, Jaycees. By no means such a huge production as Phoenix, it nevertheless gives the people of the lake country a chance to see this typical American sport in the flesh.

Chances are, by the way, that wherever a rodeo is held the bucking horses come from the mountains of eastern Montana. Each year the Mile City Jaycees stage the annual bucking-horse round-up. They track down and catch some 300 wild horses, auction them off to the big rodeo suppliers for about $10,000 gross.

On at least one occasion a Jaycee-sponsored event became even bigger than the local chapter ever intended. Several years ago the Salt Lake City Jaycees began putting on the annual Snow Cup Ski Races in December, primarily to prove to the world that there actually is good skiing in Utah that early in the season. The Snow Cup was the prime project of the big Salt Lake local, and the members really threw themselves into it. Even men like Carman Kipp, making his way up the ladder to state president while simultaneously building a successful law practice, were never too busy to serve the Snow Cup in any capacity. One year the snow was so deep that fifty Jaycees had to get out in the bitter dawn and tramp down the snow so that the skiers could have a fast track.

Thanks to such activity the Snow Cup became one of the most important meets on the international ski circuit, with the world's greatest skiers competing. And the next thing Kipp and his Jaycees knew the international organization had changed the dates of their meet from December to March—it was too important to be held that early in the season!

Just to warm these snowy pages up a bit, here's news from the Orlando, Florida, Junior Chamber, one of the world's largest. Here, each year, the Jaycees put on an orange-picking contest. It attracts a crowd of some

45,000 as pickers from Texas, Florida, and California work their way through the groves. Four Jaycees are assigned to each contestant as judges, not just to count the oranges picked, but those missed as well.

Do you know which is the world's largest basketball tournament? No, it's not the one held in Madison Square Garden, but the National Association of Intercollegiate Athletics Tournament which the Kansas City Jaycees have been putting on since 1940. The NAIA is composed of some 460 colleges throughout the country. The tournament lasts a week, and hotels for miles around are jammed with basketball fans and rooters.

In Albany, Oregon, each Fourth of July, the Jaycees stage what amounts to the World Series of woodsmanship. Thousands of fans see exciting log rolling, wood cutting, sawing contests.

The Champaign-Urbana, Illinois, Jaycees stage a speed skating contest for some 200 ice skaters each year. The winner is the National Indoor Champion.

The Jaycees of Tonawanda and North Tonawanda, New York, stage the annual Swift Water Regatta on the Niagara River. The regatta has grown to the point where it takes in several classes of speed boats and lasts for two days. In Washington the Jaycees shoot the rapids of the Columbia River each year, running the 16 miles of white water, including a waterfall, between Prosser and Benton City. Jaycees from those towns, as well as from Pasco, Grandview, and Richland participate.

While on the water, the San Diego Jaycees stage the Yellowtail Fishing Derby each year, with some 75,000 people participating, $25,000 in prizes, and well over 40,000 unlucky fish getting caught each year.

The Cambridge, Maryland, Jaycees put on a muskrat skinning contest with contestants coming from as far away as Louisiana and Canada to participate. Just in case you had forgotten, the world's record in muskrat skinning is 1:15.4 minutes for five pelts.

Another unique contest is the annual BB-gun shoot staged by the Grand Rapids, Michigan, Jaycees. At this contest over 1,500 kids blast away with their air rifles at official targets with police officers coaching. The Jaycees not only stage the tournament, but furnish the mountains of hot dogs and rivers of soda pop the kids manage to put away.

Along shooting lines, the Caldwell, Idaho, Jaycees became concerned about the growing rift between city sportsmen and farmers. More and more excellent Idaho shooting land was being closed to sportsmen because those self-same sportsmen were leaving gates open so that livestock could escape, being careless where they shot, and committing other thoughtless acts. The Jaycees staged a campaign designed to educate the hunter and conciliate the farmer, and it worked well.

And now, to close up this most partial list of Jaycee sporting activities—there are hundreds more—here is the wildest Jaycee project of all: The annual Okeene, Oklahoma, Rattlesnake Hunt!

This has been an annual affair for twenty years. It attracts well over 2,000 snake hunters. One Sunday in April, just as the snakes start coming out of their dens and into the warm sunlight, the hunters head out for

Salt Creek Canyon with their forked sticks and burlap bags. When a hunter spots a snake he pins its head to the ground with the forked stick, grabs it behind the head with his free hand, and throws it in the bag.

First-aid kits are kept handy, just in case. Getting bit is even considered something of an honor; the victims become a member of the Order of the White Fang, a most exclusive society with a built-in initiation.

The hunt is always a profitable one. At almost $50 an ounce for venom, $.50 a pound for snakes, the Okeene Jaycees do well. They sell to proprietors of zoos and snake houses, as well as to canners of that, ugh, delicacy, rattlesnake meat.

And at the end of the day, fittingly, the hunters gather round the banquet table. What do they eat? Why, deep-fat-fried rattlesnake meat, of course!

6 | CRASH LANDING AT ABBEVILLE

DOWN IN A CORNER of the stockroom at national headquarters sits a big metal file cabinet. "In that cabinet," Bob Cox told a visitor to national headquarters one day, "lies the heart of this organization."

For here are filed the digests of award-winning state and local Jaycee projects. Scores of awards are made each year, ranging from the most coveted of all, the Harold M. Marks Memorial award to the outstanding Jaycee chapter of the year on down to the winners in special categories, but all are based in part on these digests. They must be according to regulations, written in outline form, with major divisions and subheads, all neatly lettered and numbered. Yet within these crisp, concise, businesslike outlines often lies a story of suspense, drama, excitement. Here, let's reach in this top drawer and pull one out. . . .

At the top someone has drawn a big star—we have pulled out a first-place winner! The category: Aviation. Division: I (towns under 5,000 population). The outline is submitted by the Junior Chamber of Ralls, Texas, population 2,400, 49 Jaycees.

And now the story unfolds. Under "nature and purpose" of the project we see five points. Number three is "to train pilots within our club who might assist in air rescue work, be better employees because of ability to fly, provide a more convenient, faster, safer method of transportation to state and national meetings."

Under "B. Steps in completion," the plot thickens. We see, each with its several lettered sub-subheads: "1. Acquiring Airplane, 2. Learning to Fly, 3. Flying." We follow the organization of the committee, the hours spent preparing a list of available planes, then narrowing the choice down to one. We find that an instructor was secured, and the Jaycee Flying Club formed. They proceeded with ground instruction, medical examinations, and, then, glory be, "f. Learned to Fly."

But this story is not without conflict. We see it in the cryptic subhead, "1. Further Rules Were Adopted Since Everyone Wanted to Fly at Once."

However, this was soon forgotten as new developments happened thick and fast. Two local businesses bought planes, based them on the new Jaycee-developed field. One Jaycee, soon after soloing, flew his wife to a city hospital for an emergency operation. And one day a pleasantly amazed pilot from far away who had been totally unaware of the existence of the field just moments before, thankfully put his plane down on it in a dead-stick landing. His engine had conked out on him just as he had noticed the strip.

And so a letter was written to the Civil Aeronautics Authority, giving complete details, and now the Ralls International Airport is on the map!

In these days when we take travel across continents and oceans by jet-powered planes as a matter of course, few current members of the Junior Chamber, much less the general public, are aware of the great work the

Jaycees did for aviation in the twenties and thirties, or even the need for it. Yet, as the early days of the Jaycee movement coincided with the early days of aviation, it was natural, a generation ago, that those dynamic young men should further this dynamic young means of transportation.

It was Robert E. Condon, then national vice-president, who planned the first official Jaycee flight. Bob Condon was one of the most colorful Jaycees of all time. One of the original founders of the American Legion in Paris after World War I, he had come home to New York to organize the Young Men's Board of Trade and affiliate it with the National Junior Chamber. Thirty years later General Condon, who has held every rank in the U.S. Army from buck private to major general, was called upon to take over the highly responsible job of Civil Defense Commissioner for the 16 million people of the Greater New York metropolitan area. But in 1926 he was just a restless young man of twenty-nine, eager to get things done.

And one of the things he could do, he decided, would be to stage a "first" airmail flight, under Jaycee sponsorship. There was no direct airmail service between Atlanta and New York in 1926, and Condon determined to inaugurate it. A remarkably persuasive young man, Condon secured the plane and services of the great aviation pioneer, Captain Roscoe Turner. The two cities and the U.S. Post Office were eager to get in the act.

Turner's plane was the biggest ship made, a twin-engined Sikorsky which could carry several people in its enclosed cabin, plus the pilot and co-pilot in an open cockpit on the top. At five o'clock one morning a sack of airmail was placed in the plane with great ceremony, dignitaries from Atlanta and New York boarded the plane, and it took off from the red dirt runway of Candler Field. Condon, of course, as befitted his station, sat up in the cockpit with Turner.

They were flying along over the hills of northern Georgia and South Carolina, green in the early summer, when suddenly the right engine began spraying oil all over the place. Oil coated the windshield, oil coated Turner, oil coated Condon. The engine overheated and lost power. There were no stabilizers in twin-engine planes of 1926, and, despite all Captain Turner could do, the plane flew not exactly sideways, but on the diagonal, like a confused crab.

Continually wiping the oil from their goggles, Turner and Condon looked frantically below for a place to land. There was none. The plane was steadily losing altitude. They couldn't put off landing any longer. Ahead of them was a plowed field, sloping down a hillside to a ditch. On the other side of the ditch sat a farmhouse, a couple of apple trees, and a privy. The privy stuck out over a deep, dangerous gully, which ran at right angles to the ditch.

"How wide you think that ditch is?" Turner hollered at Condon.

"Seven, eight feet," Condon hollered back.

"I don't think it's that wide," Turner roared, "we'll try to jump it."

Turner brought the big plane in, set it down on the plowed field. It bumped and banged and clattered, but held together. Here came the ditch. It was every bit of eight feet wide. And on the other side of the ditch, several feet back, was a rock wall, running parallel to it. There was no way of stopping the plane, of course. They didn't fool around with brakes in 1926.

Just before they hit the ditch, Turner pulled back on the throttle and poured the gas to the struggling left engine. The big plane gave a little hop, and got over the ditch. Here came the rock wall. But the sudden burst of power from the left engine slewed the plane around to the right. The wing just cleared the rock wall. Now the plane was heading for the privy. Turner yanked back on the throttle once more, quickly, and the plane rolled into the apple trees and stopped, wings in the branches.

The oil-soaked pilot and Jaycee vice-president climbed down from the cockpit, while the dignitaries stumbled, weak-kneed, out of the cabin. They stood looking at the ditch, the gully, the rock wall, and the two small trees laden with small green apples, and tried to act as though nothing had happened.

Around the side of the house came a farmer. He had a straw hat on his head, a straw stuck in his mouth, overalls on, and he was leading a calf. He ambled up to the plane and its passengers.

"Good morning," Condon greeted him brightly. "We thought we'd drop in and get some apples for breakfast."

The farmer looked at Condon, at the other oil-soaked individual, at the passengers, at the plane, and then the apple trees.

"They ain't ripe yet," he said.

The nearest telephone, the farmer informed them,

was in the little town of Abbeville, four miles away. The delegation went to the nearest road and hitched a ride into town. While Turner ordered spare parts for the plane, Condon gave the editor of the local paper the story of the crash. He began by explaining that this was the First Airmail Flight from Atlanta to New York, sponsored by the United States Junior Chamber of Commerce.

"The United States *what?*" asked the editor.

That was all Condon needed to know. By nightfall he had rounded up a group of young men, typed out a charter for the Abbeville Junior Chamber of Commerce, and had their money in his pocket. The flight never did get to New York, but at least a new Junior Chamber was organized because of it.

Condon loved to enroll new members as well as new chapters. One night at the Chicago airport, he bunked next to a young airmail pilot, and, naturally, signed him up. Sometime later Condon heard that his new member was flying into New York to participate in the great New York–to–Paris Air Race. With such well-known aviation figures as Richard Evelyn Byrd, Roscoe Turner, and René Fonck already in New York, their planes practically ready to go, nobody gave this young man a chance of making it across the Atlantic. However, a delegation of Jaycees did go out to the field to meet him. His name was Charles A. Lindbergh.

When Condon was president of the Junior Chamber he set up the first National Aviation Committee and picked Walter Hinton to head it. Hinton had been the first man to cross the Atlantic in a flying machine, in the Navy's flight in 1919. He set out to improve what airports there were at that time. For one thing, runways were too small; the entire San Francisco field, for example, was only 1,200 by 600 feet.

Nor were airports marked. Pilots had to go down and read the name of the town on the railroad station. At Hinton's suggestion local Junior Chambers went to their airfields and spelled out the name of their town in white gravel letters fifty feet tall. From then on pilots not only knew where they were, but also, by the small letters "JC" at the end, they knew whom to thank.

Many new airports were brought into being, from scratch to completion, by the Jaycees. Typical is the Dayton Municipal Airport, dedicated by President Condon in 1926.

Today, aviation is just one of the hundreds of Jaycee projects. Los Angeles Jaycees, for example, stage an annual flying weekend in which 80 planes and 250 people participate—five times as many people, as a matter of fact, than are in the average Junior Chamber —but it's considered just another project.

Despite the success of the Jaycees aviation program in the early years, the current system of national projects and awards came about much later. The two men most responsible were Philip C. Ebeling of Dayton, Ohio, national president in 1938–39, and Thomas R. Reid, executive secretary, who later became director of the office of Civil Affairs for the Ford Motor Company.

Reid's predecessor, Marvin Hurley, had left for a new job several days before Reid took over. Formerly in radio work, Reid, then twenty-three years old, had never dictated a letter in his life before. On his first day he dictated seventy-five, to the three girls in the office and a dictating machine. That, incidentally, was the entire staff. The offices were three converted hotel rooms in St. Louis.

On payday, one of the girls brought in the payroll checks, ready for signature. She also brought in the current bank statement. There wasn't enough money in the bank to pay all four of them. Reid, a bachelor with a few dollars saved up, did the gentlemanly thing.

Reid was due in Georgia for a state meeting the following week. From there he went, on his own hook, to Orlando, Florida. Orlando's large and powerful Junior Chamber had gotten mad, withdrawn from the national organization. Reid spent a day in Orlando and settled the issue then and there to everybody's satisfaction. He came back to St. Louis with a check for Orlando's quarterly dues, enough to meet the payroll.

For months after that, whenever Reid needed money, he'd go to a large local which had dropped out, talk them into coming back in, and collect their dues on the spot.

Why were the locals dropping out? For one thing, charters were loosely written. A local Junior Chamber could belong to the state organization, to national, to both, or to neither. For another, some Junior Chambers saw little reason to belong to the national organization. If they wanted information on some project the very most they could get would be a mimeographed copy of a letter another local had written on a similar type of project. If the project was new, or if no other local had bothered to write a letter about it, there would simply be nothing available.

Remedies for both faults were in the works. Three years before national president Allen Whitfield had recognized the need for a drastic overhaul. One night in Raleigh, North Carolina, he sat up all night in his hotel room drafting an outline of a new national charter. He knew the impetus had to come from the state level and so he gave the ball to the Ohio stalwart, Phil Ebeling. Ebeling perfected the hotel room-outline, got it through the Ohio state convention, and carried it, now known as the Ohio Plan, into the national presidency in 1938.

Since then, thanks to the Ohio Plan, the Junior Chamber has been a unified organization, with all locals members of both the state and national organizations.

With direct lines of communication established, it was now possible for the national office to provide uniform service to state and local Junior Chambers. On this basis Reid went to General Robert Wood, then head of Sears Roebuck Company, for financial support for a booklet on an Americanism program, and came away with $1,000.

Ebeling carried the idea further. Why not secure sponsorship of worthwhile programs from reputable associations and companies which would derive benefit from them? He pointed out that the Junior Chamber, alone among service organizations, could guarantee action on a grass-roots level, where it counted. The Junior Chamber could get its manpower out and work-

ing; that was its reason for existence. Presented by
Ebeling and Reid, this proposal sold itself. The National Association of Fire Underwriters saw immediately the value of having the Jaycees work on fire
prevention. The Highway Safety Lighting Bureau was
eager to sponsor a better-lighting program. Something
new was added to a comprehensive safety program presented to the Liberty Mutual Insurance Company of
Boston—special awards to outstanding locals and members. The company readily bought the entire program.

And now each local had both complete instructions
on how to begin and carry through a worthwhile project and the additional incentive to do it better than
any other.

"The response from local groups was spectacular,"
Reid recalls. "Dues payments came in with letters of
appreciation and many chapters which had withdrawn
entirely or had never even belonged came in on a
paid-up basis."

So effective were the new, sponsored projects that
would-be sponsors began seeking out the Jaycees. One
of these was the Federal Bureau of Investigation,
through its director, J. Edgar Hoover. Each year,
Hoover told the Jaycees, 15,000 unidentified bodies
were buried, over 40,000 people were reported miss-
ing, and hundreds of persons became victims of am-
nesia and had no way of finding out who they were.
There was, in short, a great need for a national finger-
printing program. Would the Jaycees help sell it to
the people?

Indeed they would. R. H. Barry, of Fargo, North
Dakota, who has since become one of the most influ-

ential men in the North Central states, was national chairman of the program and got it off to a good start.

Reid and Ebeling were two of a feather in their Jaycee enthusiasm. Reid would visit Ebeling in Dayton nearly every weekend to talk current Jaycee business and future Jaycee policy. Once they met in a hotel room on Saturday afternoon and talked straight through until Sunday night.

This happy combination came at a happy time. The nation was now in a period of expanding economy after the depression. Young men now began flocking into established Junior Chambers, organizing new ones. The organization was now solid, its feet on the ground, and capable of this rapid expansion. The Junior Chamber started to boom.

During this year Ebeling and Reid brought out *Future,* the official magazine, and moved national headquarters to Chicago, where it was published. Reid at first served as editor of the magazine, and wrote some forty-one articles for it in its first year. In addition, that first year, he dictated 12,480 individual letters, wrote 206 pages of material for third-class mailings, and prepared layouts and copy for 19 booklets and manuals. At the age of twenty-four, he was given two full-time national assistants, and then he could *really* pour out the material. Much of this, of course, dealt with the growing project-and-awards program, or, as Bob Cox says, "the heart of this organization."

That Wonderful, Wonderful, Year

Each year, by the time the national convention begins, one group of sunken-eyed Jaycees, the awards committee, is ready to go home. For they will have read thousands of digests and pored through thousands of scrapbooks containing everything from fuzzy newspaper clippings to huge posters.

Nor is this just a cursory examination. "We're suspicious devils," Ted Whitney of Salt Lake City, Utah, state treasurer and an Awards Committee member for several years, said. "These locals will pull every trick in the book to win an award, and don't think we don't know it. We used to do the same things ourselves!"

And so you may well find Ted or another committee member carefully steaming a newspaper clipping describing a wonderful Jaycee project from the scrapbook page on which it was pasted, then thoughtfully reading the news on the back as a possible indication as to the date of the clipping. It may turn out to be a couple of years old—the local just keeps using it again and again.

The committee does a thorough, workmanlike job. For their labors they receive $9 per diem for five days. "And we sure need it, too," Whitney said. "I spent $500 in Los Angeles even before the convention opened. But it wasn't exactly on committee business."

The committee selects individual members for awards in four different categories. The Clayton Frost Memorial Awards go to the five outstanding state presidents. The Clint Dunagan Memorial Awards go to the ten outstanding national directors. The Seldon Waldo Memorial Awards go to five outstanding chairmen of national committees, the Wayne McCall Memorial Awards go to the outstanding international directors. It's interesting to look back over the names of the award winners of the past several years and note how many of them have become almost household names to Jaycees. Over the years some of these would include Edwin H. May, Jr., Roland Tibbetts and A. Park Shaw, Jr., of Connecticut; Frank Pasquerilla and Kenelm L. Shirk of Pennsylvania; Jack Barnes of Virginia; Jack Reich and Charles M. Shearer, Jr., of Indiana; Bob Cox of North Carolina; Irving M. Gold and A. M. Ghahremani of California; Tom Marshall of Mississippi; Dick Quinlivan of Minnesota; George C. Pagonis of New Jersey; Roy Holland of Iowa; Harry W. Hoth of Colorado; John M. King of Illinois; Howard E. Norris of Wisconsin; and Edwin F. Dosek of Nebraska.

But the individual awards are just the beginning. Each year awards are made to local and state Junior Chambers in twenty-four different categories from agriculture and conservation to state publications. Entries from locals are broken down into five different population groups, and the first three winners are named in each.

The outstanding Junior Chamber in each state wins the Henry Giessenbier Award. These winners compete on the national level for the Clarence H. Howard Memorial Award, presented to the top chapter in each of the five population divisions.

And the outstanding chapter of them all wins the Harold A. Marks Memorial Award. Usually, of course, this award is won by one of the big, powerful Junior Chambers, like St. Paul, Phoenix, Minneapolis, or Dallas, but on two occasions, smaller cities, Winston-Salem and Rocky Mount, North Carolina, have won.

And then, at the 1956 convention at Kansas City, an

announcement was made that carried the biggest impact since the report of the outcome of the David-Goliath contest. The winner of the Marks Award was Layton, Utah, *a 22-man chapter in a town of 3,000 population.*

If the Layton high school had knocked over the Baltimore Colts for the national football championship it wouldn't have been much more surprising. After all, many Junior Chambers have committees numbering twenty-two men.

What did this handful of young men do to make their chapter the best of all the Junior Chambers in the country? Well, here's a bare summary of their activities during the year.

They published their own monthly paper, *Straws in the Wind.* Their publicity committee got out regular news releases. They kept up the standard Junior Chamber activities, such as bringing in new members, and they certainly kept the old members busy. Delegates attended all the official Jaycee meetings in the state, and twenty-one of the twenty-two members attended the state convention. Eleven of the members, in yellow and white Mercurys bought especially for the occasion, attended the national convention in Atlanta. (Some *states* didn't send that many delegates.) In addition to all these business functions, they staged several social get-togethers.

The Layton Junior Chamber organized a coalition of the eight clubs in Davis County. In their extension program they put in a new chapter in a neighboring town, started on a second, and revitalized a slumbering chapter.

A continuing project was the city park. They promoted bulldozers, not to mention picks and shovels, and cleaned out a creek bottom in the town.

They put out a city directory, starting with nothing but an idea, winding up with a handsomely bound directory containing up-to-the-minute information on every resident and business in town.

They operated on what the treasurer, Wendell Philipps, called a $16,000 budget—"$8,000 in, $8,000 out."

They carried on a complete Youth Fitness program, raffling off, of all things, a trip to Alaska for first prize. They staged a Get-Out-the-Vote campaign, which resulted in the highest percentage of voting Layton ever had. They staged a turkey shoot. Their Christmas celebration was complete with outdoor lighting, baskets for indigent families, and toys and goodies for needy children. They conducted a Voice of Democracy program, put on a Youth Government Day in which the boys and girls actually ran the town. ("Best government this town's had in a long time," one of the old timers observed.) They raised money for a music scholarship for a deserving local student, and sponsored a Junior Citizens Project. They campaigned for a bond issue for new sewers. They conducted a bicycle inspection and raised money for the Olympic Fund. They ran a continuous bowling program. They put on a big Jaycee week, had a stag night, and played as hard as they worked.

In addition to the planned projects, the Layton Jaycees eagerly met emergencies as they arose. When the house of a Layton family in straitened circumstances burned down, the Jaycees pitched in and cleaned up the rubble while it was still smoking. Then they raised money for a new house and helped to erect it.

When four Vietnamese Jaycees, touring America on the way to the convention, dropped in, Layton staged a party for them. Unfortunately, the guests seemed to lose interest at an early hour. Not until the Vietnamese had been tucked, limp and snoring, into their beds did the Layton Jaycees realize they had forgotten something. Nobody had told the Vietnamese that the cold orange juice they were putting away with gusto on that hot night was laced with Vodka.

Maintaining a careful record of everything was a project in itself. The president that year, Everett A. McGhie, was a hard taskmaster on the paper work. They filled several scrapbooks, each 18 inches square and so thick you could carry but one at a time.

But we still haven't talked about the *big* projects. For example, the fine arts program, under the direction of Ken Cooper, a past president. Cooper just happened to sing in a barber-shop quartet, so his fine arts program consisted of a contest in which barber-shop quartets from all over the area competed.

Another special program was their project for clean-up, fix-up, paint-up week. The Jaycees persuaded the man who owned the town's number one eyesore, a ramshackle old frame house, to let them burn it down. They promised to clean up the mess afterward. Amid great fanfare, they ignited the tinder-dry walls. It was a beautiful conflagration, all right, and people came from miles around to see it.

But when the flames and smoke had cleared away,

the Layton Jaycees stood there gawking. All that frame had been just a veneer over adobe walls. Before their eyes stood a smoke-blackened mud structure, more horrible to look at than ever.

And they were honorbound to tear it down.

The Jaycees worked a solid week, after hours and all weekend, knocking down those stone-hard walls, shoveling the debris in trucks they'd scrounged, hauling it off to the city dump.

One of the Jaycees who worked as hard as anybody was Wendell Philipps, the treasurer. Wendell suffered from a chronic heart condition, but he knocked down walls and shoveled adobe with the best of them.

"But that work didn't bother me at all compared to the way I felt the day before Riata Day," Wendell said later. "It was my job to get $300 worth of nickels, dimes, and quarters. The minute before the bank closed, I walked up to the teller, big as life, and poked a check for $300 at him. My heart was hammering so I could hardly get my breath. He gave me the money, and I took off like a jet. Because we didn't have no $300 in that bank."

There is no question in the mind of any man, woman, or child, or, for that matter, any living thing in or near Layton, as to when Riata Day begins. It begins at 6 A.M. on the Fourth of July, when the Reveille Committee sets off six 9-inch mortars.

By the time the people have stopped shaking, at seven o'clock, it's time for the Chuck Wagon breakfast. The Jaycees have been up since dawn, preparing a hearty western breakfast—ham, eggs, biscuits—in carload lots. They block off the main drag of the town, and feed not only the entire population of Layton, but everybody traveling through as well. Cars from twenty-three states and five Canadian provinces stopped by that morning.

So did a Greyhound bus. Some of the passengers wondered why it was necessary to have a breakfast stop so soon, having left Salt Lake City just a half hour before. They were given several reasons, but here's the real one: The driver of the bus was a Layton Jaycee.

Ken Cooper was chairman of Riata Day, as he was twelve other programs. He was also a director. Lamar Day, vice-president, had several more. All in all, the Layton local conducted seventy-three projects that year. Many coincided. You'd be chairman of a committee one day, just another member of a different committee the next.

Every now and then today the Jaycees who were active that year get together at chapter headquarters and talk about it. They all say that they worked harder that year than any year before or since. But you can tell, from the reminiscent, sad little smiles on their faces, that there's not one of them who wouldn't give a lot to live it all over again, that wonderful year when the twenty-two young men from Layton won the highest award in Jayceedom.

7 | *THE BIG ISSUES*

IN THE GRIMY INDUSTRIAL AREA of a big graft-ridden city, a young man with a smile frozen on his face but fear in his heart is bumped and jostled by a bunch of toughs, hissing obscene threats in his ears. . . . Another young man begins to notice the same faces wherever he goes, and suddenly realizes he's being followed. . . . Still another young man learns that he is marked for extinction by the underworld. "Someday," a character in the know says darkly, "they're going to find that guy's body at the bottom of the bay."

Characters in television whodunits? Not on your life. These young men are all Jaycees, doing what they consider to be their duty in spite of danger, threats, and proffered bribes. They typify the new trend in Jaycee activity. For all over the country, on local, state and national levels, Jaycees are becoming more and more active in the real issues and conflicts of American life.

"The Jaycees have come of age," is the way Ben Swanson, executive vice-president, puts it. "This is no longer an organization devoted to planting trees in city parks—although we certainly intend to continue that important part of our program. But over and beyond our do-good projects, today, no matter where you go, you find increasing Jaycee activity in the field of non-partisan political activity, direct interest and participation in government. Nor does this mean more get-out-the-vote type projects. We're going beyond that. For you don't have to drag an educated and informed citizen to the polls—if he knows and understands the issues, he's there ahead of you. It is only through this great movement of educated, interested, and alert citizens that we will stem the tide of creeping socialism, guarantee to each and every person the only real security that exists, the security of your own personal ability."

Although this eager determination to plunge heavily into controversial issues has picked up momentum in recent years, Jaycees have long been moving in this direction. In the earliest days of the organization, long before most states enacted laws against usury, the Jaycees dared take up the cudgel against those sleazy operators, the loan sharks.

In 1934, long before most citizens of the United States fully realized the dangers of communism, the young Junior Chamber, at the Miami convention, went on record *"denouncing and opposing the methods and objectives of the Communist Party and affiliated organizations, and hereby recommend the adoption of a program in opposition thereto."*

The Get-Out-and-Vote Committee had been active even before then. In 1932 the Jaycees put on a stunt which focused national attention on the importance of the right to vote. With newsreel cameras grinding out their record of the big day, the world's champion parachute jumper, Joe Crane, dressed in colonial wig and knee breeches, jumped out of an autogiro above Roosevelt Field, New York. Courtlandt Otis, of New York, national Jaycee president, was waiting with other national figures on the field. The parachutist landed, struggled up to the waiting delegation and, somewhat breathlessly, read from a scroll the words of Ben Franklin: "The right to vote marks the free man from the slave."

Then he added, "And now, for God's sake, help me get this damned thing off."

In the 1940 convention at Washington, the Junior Chamber passed a resolution which had a greater impact upon the nation than any other activity in Jaycee history. This was an important year. Abroad a war that was soon to become world-wide was raging. At home a large and voluble but misguided segment of people was attempting to hamstring American preparedness. The bill before Congress proposing a peacetime draft was under particularly bitter fire. It all came to a focal point in the nation's capital. In that seething atmosphere the Jaycees began their twenty-first convention. And if Congress was in an uproar over the proposed draft act, imagine the scene on the convention floor when a resolution approving it was introduced. For here at this convention were the very young men who would be directly subject to such a draft. The whole nation looked on to see what action they would take.

It was a Southern delegate who summed up the Jaycee consensus of opinion. Speaking from the floor, he cried, "Ah don't want to go to wah any more than anybody else, but if it turns out ah got to go, then, by God, teach me how to fight!"

And the resolution was passed, passed by the young men whom it directly concerned.

And later that year the Congress of the United States

made the draft act law—by the margin of one vote.
There is no question but that the Jaycee resolution
made a strong impression on the legislators. And think
of what might have happened had the country not had
that period of preparedness before war did come!

When war came, Walter W. Finke of Minneapolis
was president; Douglas Timmerman, of St. Joseph,
Missouri, who had resigned as elected vice-president to
take the job, was executive vice-president. They asked
themselves this question: What would be the Junior
Chamber's wartime role?

An emergency meeting of the executive board was
called. It split into two camps. One group was for dis-
banding the organization entirely. The other group,
led by Finke and Timmerman, maintained that Jaycees
could accomplish much more as an organization than
as individuals.

Their side won. And then the work began. As Jaycees poured into the armed services, locals were deci-
mated, left leaderless. One Junior Chamber had seven
presidents in one year. This meant even more travel
than usual on the part of the top executives in order to
hold the locals together. But travel was not easy in wartime. Many a time the president of the U.S. Junior
Chamber of Commerce had to hitchhike from town to
town to make his visitations.

But surely it was worth it. Every Junior Chamber
made positive contributions to the war effort; many
were almost unbelievable. In Bluefield, West Virginia,
Jaycees organized a physical-training program for members who had been rejected by the Armed Forces for
physical reasons. It was open to anyone. At times the

program included over 100 men, all knocking themselves out in order to build themselves up and get in
the Army.

The Honolulu Jaycees did a particularly magnificent
job. They organized 30,000 school children and ran a
monster scrap drive. They worked out a way to make
wall boards for Army and Navy installations right
there on the island out of local materials, saving twenty
tons of shipping space from the mainland a month.

In Iowa, the Jaycees got out and shucked the corn,
in Washington they picked apples, in Nebraska they
harvested potatoes and sugar beets. In Oklahoma City
they raised a million dollars in war bonds in four hours.
In Danville, Virginia, the Jaycees operated a pre-flight
training school for the Air Force—the only such course
not run by an educational institution.

Everywhere they helped servicemen. They built pick-
up stations outside hundreds of towns, arranged transportation, dances—you name it, they did it. In Joplin,
Missouri, they scrounged building material and put up
a bunkhouse. One night it housed 120 servicemen.

In 1943 the Jaycee tide began to turn. Disabled
veterans were returning from the armed services, and
they joined the Jaycees to continue fighting the war
in the only way left to them, on the home front. In the
last years of the war, as the Junior Chamber grew
stronger and its contributions greater, there was no
longer any question but that the Jaycees had made the
right decision.

During the war and immediately after it, there was
much talk of the Four Freedoms—freedom from want,
freedom from fear, freedom from hunger, freedom of

worship. John Ben Shepperd, of Gladewater, Texas—
he has since served as attorney general of Texas—one
of the Junior Chamber's most colorful presidents,
thought there should be a fifth freedom—the freedom
of opportunity.

John Ben had toured Europe in the aftermath of
war, had noted the alarming loss of this fifth freedom
in the trend to socialism. He resolved to fight this trend
in his own country. He dreamed up one of the Junior
Chamber's most dramatic and publicized projects, the
Fifth Freedom Flight.

He managed to charter a twin-engine plane, set up
an itinerary by which he'd visit twenty-nine states in
thirty-three days. He took with him Frank Fister, executive vice-president and a former Utah state Jaycee president, reporters, photographers, and a load of fine ten-
gallon hats. He personally presented twenty-four of
these hats to twenty-four state governors, and the
twenty-fifth, the very finest of all, to President Harry
S. Truman in the White House.

"It was a fascinating trip, all right," Frank Fister
recalled later. "But then, John Ben was a fascinating
guy. He's the kind of person you like to do things for.
John Ben could be talking to a group of fellows, mention idly that he was hungry, and they'd all start fighting to take him to dinner. He gained fifty pounds during his term as president. He was always grabbing a
piece of pie and a glass of milk, then dashing up to his
hotel room to clean his teeth. He got so fat he got stuck
in a taxicab in Rio de Janeiro during the JCI World
Congress, so he went on a diet and got back to normal."

Naturally, wherever John Ben and the Freedom
Flight went, something happened. He was in Wyoming

for the dedication of the new state university field house at Laramie. A top professional entertainer had been brought in to star. Governor Lester C. Hunt of Wyoming introduced John Ben, who made a couple of good-humored cracks about Wyoming. So Governor Hunt, who was pretty good, too, said a few things about Texas. John Ben arose for the rebuttal. The crowd loved it and called for more. The professional never did go on.

John Ben had adventures all across the country. He got in a row with Ernest Hemingway and took Ralph Bellamy in a crap game at Sun Valley, Idaho. A couple of days later one of the plane's tires went flat, and for a week the pilot took off and landed on one wheel. Nor could fog over Lake Michigan stop the Fifth Freedom Flight. . . . It continued on, fifty feet over the water, with Governor Kim Sigler of Michigan following in a single-engined plane.

In Maine, the plane flew through the smoke of forest fires to install a new chapter at Bar Harbor. The governor of Maine was there too, of course. Next day the fire spread to Bar Harbor, and the new Jaycees took on the important job of evacuating the panic-stricken community as their first project.

When the flight ended John Ben was completely bushed. But it was worth it: the Fifth Freedom Flight had delivered its important message to the American people.

You Can't Buy the Junior Chamber!

Strangely enough, one of the Junior Chamber's most controversial, even bitter campaigns, came about in a most innocent, almost naive way. The President of the

United States, Harry S. Truman, a Democrat, had asked a previous President, Herbert Hoover, a Republican, to investigate the entire government organization and to make recommendations for its improvement. The Hoover Commission proposed a complete reorganization which would mean better government at far less cost. The Jaycees voted the promotion of the Hoover Report as their number one project for the year 1949–50.

And then the storm broke. It seemed that the Hoover Report would upset too many gravy trains. Entrenched governmental agencies saw in its proposals for streamlined efficiency a threat to their size, payroll, and importance. Bitter opposition came from the veterans organizations, which felt that proposals went too far in reducing costs of veterans' hospitals and individual benefits.

Naturally, of course, a large proportion of the Jaycees themselves were veterans. Many of its members were also members of veterans organizations; General Bob Condon, former Jaycee president, had been one of the founders of the American Legion and was a lifetime member. General Olmsted was another former Jaycee president and prominent legionnaire. The Jaycees wanted no fight with so kindred an organization. At the same time, they had voted to promote the Hoover Report, and, further, a re-examination of the issues gave no reason to reconsider. The Jaycees went into action.

Not long after that Clifford D. Cooper, the talented executive who headed the Junior Chamber that year, received a hush-hush invitation to a special meeting of top industrialists. A concrete offer was tendered him: If he called off Jaycee support for the Hoover Report, he could write his own ticket.

Cooper swallowed. "I'm sorry, gentlemen," he said, "but the Junior Chamber has directed me to work for the objectives of the Hoover Report. I couldn't do otherwise even if I wanted to."

Not long after, it became obvious to Cooper that he was being tailed. He learned that private investigators were combing his background, looking for dirt.

Cooper went right on speaking for the Hoover Report. So did his executive vice-president, Robert Ladd, one of the Junior Chamber's most efficient administrators. So did Junior Chamber spokesmen all across the nation. They flooded Congress with mail. A special delegation of Jaycees visited the capital. Fifteen senators and thirty-eight representatives met with the delegation, and were impressed by the young men's earnestness. And still the Jaycee-inspired mail poured in. "This," the venerable Senator George of Georgia said candidly, "is the most effective job that's ever been done on me."

Eventually, 84 per cent of the provisions of the Hoover Report became law, with ensuing benefits to all the people of the nation.

Mr. Hoover himself was so impressed by the Jaycees support that he made his first public appearance in years, addressing the 1950 convention at Chicago and giving full credit to the magnificent job they had done.

The Jaycee work on the Hoover Report had an interesting aftermath. A national institution, seeking a way to get a nonpartisan project over to the public, kept hearing about the terrific job the Jaycees had done from members of Congress. Through Ted Anderson, the colorful Salt Lake City Jaycee vice-president assigned to public relations, arrangements were made to sponsor the highly successful Jaycee project, Operation Tax Reform. This was a broad program, stimulating individual study of the current tax structure so as better to understand its inequities and penalties on individual enterprise.

To call public attention to the need for tax reform, Anderson sent a modern Paul Revere on a ride from the West Coast to Washington, gathering signatures to a tax reform petition as he went.

A young Alaskan Jaycee, Maurice "Mike" Gravel, was selected to be the modern Paul Revere.

Mike had adventures all across the country, but perhaps his worst moment occurred in Salt Lake City before national chairman Anderson and thousands of onlookers. After securing Governor George D. Clyde's signature on the petition, at the state capitol, he was to ride on horseback down steep State Street to the business district. A spirited horse was borrowed from the sheriff's posse. Mike bravely scrambled aboard. The parade started immediately, Mike at the head, followed by dignitaries in the official Tax Reform Rambler, more automobiles, then more horses. It hadn't gone far before it was obvious that oversights had been made.

For one thing, it was sleeting, and the steep incline was covered with ice. The horse began picking up speed.

For another thing, nobody had asked if Mike knew how to ride a horse. He didn't. The deputy who owned the horse had been forgotten and left at the tail end of the parade. He saw what was happening and began running up to the front, hollering. The people in front of him thought he was telling them to go faster, and so they did, pushing the Rambler right up on the horse's tail. That did it. The horse put on the brakes. It spread its legs and locked them, and went into a slide. Mike went over the saddle, up between the horse's ears. And that's how Operation Tax Reform entered Salt Lake City.

Despite such mishaps, Mike delivered the signatures to the Congress of the United States, as per schedule, in a fitting ceremony.

From Dying City to Murder Town

Most people, with a picture of a group of Jaycees planting trees in their minds, would have some difficulty picturing these same young men in a grim and desperate battle against the thugs and hoodlums of a graft-ridden and corrupt city government. Most Americans, as a matter of fact, living in typical towns across the land, would have difficulty imagining the sordid situation which made this fight necessary.

It happened in Newark, New Jersey, in the early fifties. Though Newark's population numbered close to half a million, this was a dying city. It was getting to the point that Newark wasn't safe for decent people to live in or work in. Property taxes were the highest in the nation, and on top of that actual extortion was being practiced on legitimate businesses of the city. When a reputable business is being highjacked in such fashion, when it can't even guarantee its employees protection on their way to work, it might as well move out. That's just exactly what many firms did.

And so did the good citizens. As they fled to the suburbs, more riffraff poured in. Finally it came to the point that two of the biggest employers of the city, the Mutual Life Insurance Company—of which former Jaycee president H. Bruce Palmer was president—and the Prudential Life Insurance Company, both with roots deep in Newark, had actually chosen property out of the city for relocation. That would really be the end of the town.

The odds against saving Newark seemed impossible, and yet the Newark Junior Chamber, in foolhardy desperation, determined to try. The amazing thing is that of the ninety members of the Chamber, no more than ten still resided in the city limits.

How could the city be saved? First the Jaycees, along with other civic groups, tried to change to a city-manager form of government. The machine herded its people to the polls and beat the proposal down.

The Jaycees almost quit. After all, why beat your head against a stone wall? Why fight for people who haven't the sense even to know you're fighting for them? But, as Ben Swanson has pointed out, if you can't take one defeat, you're not a leader. And these young men were leaders. Again they tried. This time they worked for a strong-mayor type of city government as opposed to the commission system, and this time they were successful.

But their success meant nothing unless they could get a strong and honest man for mayor. A screening committee was set up. Their choice was Leo P. Carlin, union official and incumbent commissioner, whose personal honesty had remained unimpeachable even in such surroundings. In Leo P. Carlin lay Newark's last chance.

One of the Jaycees active during this entire period was Walter W. Weller, Jr., a quiet, earnest young man from a quiet, respectable background. Walt Weller was probably the last man in the world you'd expect to find standing outside a company gate at quitting time, handing out campaign literature. Yet there he was, night after night, taking the bumping and jostling, hearing obscene threats. Like the other Jaycees he always parked his car several blocks away. He could risk personal injury, but he couldn't afford to buy a new car!

And sometimes, standing in these dreary surroundings, fighting against such hopeless odds, he wondered what he was doing there in the first place. He didn't even live in Newark. He didn't have to work there. The only answer was that he knew in his heart that what he was doing was right.

Thanks to men like Walt, the miracle happened. Carlin was elected. He began cleaning up the city. Bruce Palmer's Mutual Life and the Prudential decided to stay on, building handsome new edifices in the heart of town. Other industries began moving in. And Newark, once a dying city, came back.

In the meantime, far to the south, other Jaycees were carrying on another battle against city evil. Led by Martin Zindler, the Houston Jaycees were fighting murder. Their city had the highest per capita murder rate in the country; it was getting to be known as Murdertown, U.S.A.

They organized a crime study group, visited similar groups in other cities, flew to Washington for FBI guidance. First concrete act was to get the city council to outlaw the sale of switch-blade knives. The Houston Crime Commission was established with a full-time director, and full support of the city. That's when the underworld began muttering dark threats against Zindler, the spearhead, saying, "Someday they're going to find that guy at the bottom of the bay."

But Zindler kept going. And today Houston is no longer Murdertown, U.S.A.

Big Defeat, Bigger Victory

This is the story of a Jaycee project which failed. Yet it was a glorious failure, in a sense, if only because it was such a stupendous undertaking. For this is a story of how the Jaycees tried to change the entire legislative setup of the whole big state of Texas....

The story begins at, of all places, a birthday party in Midland, Texas. Hulon Brown, Midland Jaycee, attorney and member of the Texas state legislature, was there. And somehow, when the conversation got around to politics, Hulon found himself right in the middle of it.

"Sometimes I'm ashamed to be a member of the Texas state legislature," he was saying bitterly. "The way it's set up, a man has got to be either rich, crooked, or stupid to serve. Do you know the salary of a Texas state legislator? I'll tell you—$1,200 for the entire two-year term. What do those two years cost him? At least $10,000! Who makes up that difference, and more besides? In too many cases it's the lobbyists, the influence groups. Many times their interest is not the public interest. Who loses? The public."

Brown went on to tell how a state legislator could get anything he wanted for his vote—money, power, whisky, women. It was common knowledge that certain tables in the hotel dining rooms were reserved by lobbyists. Sit at one of them, eat your fill, get up and go. The check is automatically taken care of.

"The whole thing is cock-eyed," Brown went on. "Do you realize that 1,600 bills are introduced at each session of the legislature? You can't read, much less understand, 1,600 bills in 120 days. Meeting only once every two years, we must plan the entire budget of the state of Texas thirty months in advance. Imagine a thing like that on a national level. If a war broke out you might have to wait a year to appropriate the money to fight it! What a hell of a way to run the biggest state in the nation!"

Hulon paused for breath. One of the young women who had been listening asked, a little timidly, "Aren't you a Jaycee, Hulon?"

"Sure," Hulon said. "What's that got to do with it?"

"Well, nothing," the young woman said, "only except if it's all that bad I think the Jaycees would be just the people to do something about it."

Hulon stared at her for a moment. "By God, you're right!" he breathed.

Hulon Brown turned and tossed in excitement all that night. Next day was Friday, Jaycee luncheon day. Hulon stood up in front of his fellow members and, in a powerful speech, called on the Junior Chamber to work for a change in the Texas state legislature. A special meeting was held immediately, and a resolution to that effect put through.

A regional conference was scheduled in Amarillo that very weekend. Brown was there and got his resolution through. He attended five more regional conferences on successive weekends, selling his program at each one. Next week was the state convention at Brownsville, 700 miles away, and he sold it there, too. It became the Texas Jaycees' number one project.

The proposal called for annual meetings of the legislature, and a salary in line with other states of equal population—$7,500 per year plus adequate expenses. For this to become law it would have to pass both houses of the legislature, then go to the people of Texas for final approval in the form of an amendment to the Constitution.

The Jaycees went all out in typical fashion, with kits, brochures, petition forms, sample publicity releases, car stickers—the works.

It soon became obvious that this project was unlike any other. Jaycees, as a rule, don't meet positive resistance. Who's against a Christmas party for orphans, or more flowers in the park?

But this was no Christmas party. One legislator told his hometown Jaycees bluntly, "The lobbyists are going to spend a million bucks to beat this bill, and it's going to take more than the Texas Jaycees to pass it."

Opposition came from unexpected quarters. Many big corporations and trade groups, surprisingly, opposed it. Why? "Because," one of their spokesmen said bluntly, "when we can buy legislators we know where we stand."

Even reputable businessmen who would not stoop to bribery opposed the change. "The more often they meet, the more taxes they slap us with," one explained.

For the first time individual Jaycees were expressly forbidden by their employers to work on a Jaycee project. Some rebelled and worked anyway, and Jaycees were fired in Texas because of it.

Nor did the Jaycees themselves stick together. "You fellows mean well," drawled one Jaycee who was also a member of the legislature, "but you aren't paying me."

Another Jaycee legislator responded to all the mailings with glowing letters, all the while actively campaigning against the measure.

Dr. Douglas Guthrie, Jr., Texas state president for 1958–59, was naturally eager to make the number one project a success. It's safe to say that no other state president has run into such solid opposition so soon.

Doug, an earnest, friendly young man, went into the campaign with no first-hand knowledge of the issues. He went to the capitol to see for himself.

"In just five minutes I knew we were right," he said later. "Frankly, I was disgusted with my own state legislature, my own people. Those people weren't even making an effort to govern the state of Texas."

Doug learned something else at the state capitol. The capitol correspondents requested a press conference. Doug, naturally, acquiesced. Don't Jaycees and reporters always work together? But this was a brand-new experience. These weren't the friendly, relaxed reporters the Jaycee usually sees. These men asked penetrating, searching questions, and they weren't all friendly. When they got through with him he was soaking wet with perspiration. And when the stories came out, oh, brother!

For the first time, Doug began hearing serious criticism of the Junior Chamber. This was a matter of grave importance. Were the Texas Jaycees right, he asked himself, to involve the Junior Chamber in politics?

"Well," Guthrie said grimly, after he had thought the whole thing through, "if we, the honest, patriotic young business and professional men of this nation don't get into politics, then just who in the hell will? I believe that Jaycees have a moral obligation to our community, state, and nation, to the world, for that matter, to do the best we can, wherever we can. If that's controversial, so be it.

"But there's more to it than that. The Junior Chamber is not a cemetery, something that only takes and never gives. I believe that the Junior Chamber has an obligation to its individual members just as its members have an obligation to the Junior Chamber. Doug Guthrie has but a small individual voice, but with a large organization that voice can be heard more widely. And I believe that the Junior Chamber of Commerce owes me and all other Jaycees its support in making our voices heard in just and worthwhile causes."

The Jaycees learned early that politics is not a game played by rules. After being tricked a couple of times, they played some tricks of their own. For example, during one period their bill was bottled up in committee. Four of the seven members were opposed to it. One day one of those four was away from the capitol. The Jaycees quickly arranged a luncheon for another member of the opposition, and saw to it that the beer flowed copiously. The committee was hastily convened, and with the vote three to two in favor, the bill cleared the committee.

More politicking was necessary to get it through the House and Senate. Then it went before the people in a Constitutional referendum. With the chips down, competition got stiffer. Under pressure from big advertisers, newspapers which had approved the program now opposed it. False and misleading statements were played up in a deliberate effort to confuse the people. And they were effective. For the Constitutional amendment was defeated.

"But we gained many things even in defeat," Doug Guthrie said. "Our organization gained stature, our members benefited through participation. More of us are dedicated to better government today than ever before simply because now we know the score. God knows we learned it the hard way. And with this knowledge one of these days we'll win."

The Jaycees may have lost their battle in the biggest state in the union in 1958, but they won in the biggest state in the union in 1959. And so, this is the story of a victory. . . .

Some might say this story begins in 1741, when a Dane named Vitus Bering saw land and discovered Alaska, or in 1867, when the United States bought that land for seven million dollars. To Jaycees, however, the story begins with the formation of the Gastineau Junior Chamber in Fairbanks, Alaska. For this meeting brought into the Junior Chamber a supercharged young attorney named Edward A. Merdes.

Merdes, a graduate of the Cornell University Law School, was then assistant attorney general. One day a friend of his, Henry Camerot, another young live wire, suggested to Ed that they organize a Junior Chamber of Commerce. Ed, he recalls today, almost refused. "I had the idea that this was a kind of stepchild of the Senior Chamber," he says. "But Henry showed me a list of young men he had already approached, and some of them I knew to be fellows of great ability. So I went along, too."

Ed started blasting his way up the Jaycee ladder immediately. Even among Alaskans, who, most of them, have proved their ability to overcome inertia by leaving their home town and coming to Alaska in the first place, Merdes was a standout. When he was elected president of the Alaska Jaycees in 1957, he set Alaska's sights on the highest goal attainable—position of number one in the parade of states.

To lead the parade, every single Junior Chamber in the Jaycee state must do its level best. Any one local chamber can mess up the whole thing just by not knocking itself out. Ed and his fellow officers determined that that would never happen.

First of all, there was the communication problem. Alaska is not only big, it's drafty. Some chapters are nearly a thousand miles apart, as far apart as New York and St. Louis. Yet they have to keep in contact with each other. But how? Travel by land most of the year is impossible; air service, though good, is expensive. (In spite of this, Ed himself traveled 30,000 miles that year.) Long distance calls are expensive, too, and everybody knows that letters are answered promptly only by the most enthusiastic and dedicated of people. And then Ed got an idea: What about the ham radio operators—those amateurs who communicate with each other by short wave?

And that's how the Alaska Jaycee short-wave communication system came to be set up. It was highly effective. Jaycee jabber filled the Arctic air waves. And so, at the 1958 convention, Alaska, least likely of all the states, led the parade.

But that wasn't all the Alaskan Jaycees were accomplishing. They, like most Alaskans, wanted with patriotic fervor to be a real part of the United States of America. The Jaycees took the lead in working for Alaskan statehood. They worked with other national and local organizations in Alaska, getting resolutions passed, arranging for follow-ups, attending to all the details.

But they knew that the real results would be obtained not by pressure from Alaska, but from the forty-eight states. And so the Alaska Jaycees took their cause to their fellow Jaycees in the other states. Just one example: The president of the Fairbanks local wrote individual personal letters to all Jaycee state presidents outlining a procedure to get word down through the locals to individual members so that they could petition their congressmen for Alaskan statehood. This was highly effective, as were other plans. Thanks to the cohesive, close-knit network of Junior Chambers in Alaska, they really blanketed the nation.

Then came the Los Angeles convention in July, 1958. The Alaskan Jaycees roared in, hard-driving, efficient, enthusiastic. They were the number one state

in the Jaycee union. They swept in their state president, big Ed Merdes, as the first national vice-president
from Alaska. And every one of those Alaska Jaycees was
a lobbyist for Alaskan statehood. They buttonholed
Jaycees from every state and sold them Alaska.

And when a Jaycee is sold, he acts. A fresh flood of
letters, telegrams, and long distance calls poured in on
U.S. senators and representatives from important communities and constituents all over the forty-eight states.

And just two weeks after the Los Angeles convention,
the bill went through Congress—Alaska was the forty-
ninth state in the Union!

Other Jaycee groups have also been active in non-
partisan political activity. In St. Louis, for example,
where the whole thing began in the first place, the
Jaycees have been working for the consolidation of city
and county governments. With its ninety-eight separate
municipalities in St. Louis County, there is absolutely
no traffic control, no planning, no zoning, no coordina-
tion between police and other government agencies
from town to town.

"It's going to be a long, hard struggle," Granville J.
Haven, St. Louis president, said grimly, "but we're not
going to quit until we've got it licked."

In Shreveport, Louisiana, the Jaycees took on the
city council in a head-to-head battle. The city council
had refused to allow a city-wide referendum on a federal housing and slum clearance proposition. The Jaycees insisted that if there is one right the American
citizen has it's the right to vote, circulated a petition,
and forced the city fathers to reconsider.

"Other Jaycee projects may be bigger, and further

along," Louisiana state president Thomas F. Ruffin, said, "but what we're proudest of here in Louisiana is the way the Jaycees are wading into non-partisan political issues."

The fifty-first Jaycee state, the District of Columbia, carries on the loneliest fight. Living and working in the nation's capital, Washington Jaycees have seen Alaska and Hawaii gain statehood, including the right to send their senators and congressmen to Washington. Yet in Washington itself, the people can't even vote for dog catcher, much less mayor, city council, or even for President. The Washington Jaycees have managed to get a bill which would give these disenfranchised Americans the right to vote to the floor of the Senate again and again, and maybe, someday, it will get farther.

Operation Free Men

With the ferment of activity increasing all over the nation, with special interest coming from President Cox and Executive Vice-president Swanson at national headquarters, it became essential that the Junior Chamber have a national program. But who would head it up?

The answer came from Wichita, Kansas. There, by coincidence, just as the Junior Chamber decided that the government of Wichita could stand improvement, its president, Edwin B. Law, was approached by two men interested in setting up a citizens group. Would he and the Jaycees be interested in coming along?

"Would we? Just try and keep us out!" Law said.

Law and the Jaycee civic affairs committee felt the

Jaycees could do a better job by working with a larger group than as a strictly Jaycee operation. They then provided the framework and the impetus for such an organization, and called it Civic Progress, Inc. After two years of patient groundwork it became obvious that Civic Progress, Inc. would have to run its own candidates for the city commission in order to get results. Three vacancies on the commission would be filled in the 1959 election. Ed Law and his committee interviewed some fifty candidates, selected the three top men. The old guard fought back with every trick in the book, but the Jaycee Civic Progress candidates won by big majorities.

It was to Ed Law of Wichita, then, that national headquarters went for a national chairman of the Legislative Affairs Committee. Ed and his committee proposed a sweeping new project—*Operation Free Men.*

The revolutionary new project furnishes information and inspiration on non-partisan political activity to local Junior Chambers and sets up a system of incentives.

"The basic concept of *Operation Free Men,*" wrote Law in his official prospectus, "is the development within our membership of a personal participation at whatever political level may be of interest. We have in the past avoided this area due to its unpleasant implication and attendant hazards. We are a group of maturing men and therefore must now face true responsibility."

8 | *THE BEST WORK OF LIFE*

IT WAS SPRING in Milwaukee just after World War II, and Jaycee convention time. The city was filled with young men from all over the nation. By day they were serious, working, planning, listening attentively to the wise words of national dignitaries. But night was the time for fun, and these young people took advantage of every minute of it. Day after busy day, night after hectic night—when would it end?

Drinking it all in, from its fresh and eager beginnings right up until the final dramatic moment when the losing presidential candidate, magnificent in defeat, pledged his support to the victor, was a fresh-faced young neophyte named C. William Brownfield from Columbus, Ohio. These were the most moving days in Bill Brownfield's life. And back home, as he went about his business, phrases reminiscent of that inspiring, exciting week kept popping into his head. One day he wrote them all down. What he wrote has since been officially endorsed as the Jaycee Creed, which follows:

We believe:

That faith in God gives meaning and purpose to human life;

That the brotherhood of man transcends the sovereignty
   of nations;
That economic justice can best be won by free men
   through free enterprise;
That government should be of laws rather than of men;
That earth's great treasure lies in human personality;
And that service to humanity is the best work of life.

Jaycees all over the world have found in this creed
the words to live by. Many have followed its precepts to
positions of national and international importance, but
most Jaycees have been content to carry on "the best
work of life" on their own community level.

Often, therefore, as in 1958, community development has been marked as the number one project of the
year.

It's amazing how many opportunities to serve a man
can find in his own home town, if he but looks. Many
a man, looking, has changed the face of many a community. Cecil Edmonds of West Memphis, Arkansas,
for example. Dan Kahle, of Atlanta, Georgia. Or Ralph
Nading Hill, of Burlington, Vermont. . . . Men who
have found something that needs to be done and have
thrown themselves into it heart and soul.

Cecil Edmonds had no idea that morning he was
asked, as president of the West Memphis Jaycees, to
come take a look at the public library what a drastic
change this was going to make in his life. He expected a
handsome, dignified building, filled with books containing the wisdom of the world. For, after all, West
Memphis was a thriving, industrial city of 19,000 people, and its library should be a true reflection of it.

But what Edmonds saw was a grimy little building

that had formerly been a cheap cafe. It was both dirty
and deserted. The few books it contained were out-
moded and battered. Its total circulation was about
twelve books a month.

From then on all Cecil Edmonds cared about, outside of working hours, was the West Memphis public
library. His goal was to establish a library worthy of the
town, and he wasn't going to stop until he attained it.

He established a special library project, with himself,
of course, as chairman. With fellow Jaycees and other
civic-minded individuals, against bitter opposition of
businessmen and property owners, he got the city council to raise taxes for the specific purpose of supporting
a library. A public referendum was called and, with
Edmonds pushing and prodding, the people of West
Memphis actually approved the proposal to tax themselves more money. With this and money he raised elsewhere, Edmonds purchased books and increased library
services.

But the building, even newly painted, was still an
eyesore. So Edmonds sold the city government on building a new one. Now the opposition really got tough.
Injunctions halted construction several times. Edmonds
had to carry the case all the way up to the state attorney
general before the library was finished. It was a three
year battle.

In the meantime, Edmonds was expanding his hori-
zon. The more Edmonds fought for a library in his
own community, the more he became convinced of the
importance of the library to every community in the
world. A public library gives every town a potential
university within its own city limits. It is an integral

part of education. During the school year it supple-
ments the work of the public schools with an inte-
grated book program; during the summer, it provides
comprehensive reading programs, instructive, entertaining. The public library throws up a sturdy bul-
wark against the vicious so-called comic books. It en-
ables people to continue their education throughout
their lives.

So Edmonds took his library crusade to the state
level. He bulldozed it through there, too. Before he
got through, all forty-four Junior Chambers in Arkansas were participating in Operation Library. It was the
first 100 per cent project in the state.

Next he took on the national organization. The
Board of Directors of the United States Junior Chamber listened to him, agreed that Operation Library had
possibilities, and made it a national project on the
Class Three level.

Edmonds hit the ceiling. In a few thousand words he
told the Jaycees that Operation Library would be a
Class One project or nothing at all. The 300-man board
quailed before this one-man cyclone, reconsidered, and
made it a Class One project. Edmonds resigned as national director to become national chairman of Operation Library. Under his direction, in its very first year,
Jaycees contributed more in time and money to the
libraries of America through Operation Library than
did the federal government.

There was already some precedent for this work—
the Jaycees of Bellingham, Washington, for example.
When the city built a new library it couldn't get its
books moved from the old building into the new at any

price. For the first floor of the old building was just fifty-seven steps above the street—a long walk for anybody carrying a box of books. The Jaycees took over and built a cable-car contraption, powered by a screeching winch, which hauled the books from library to street. Forty volunteers, working until midnight for ten nights in a row, moved more than 60,000 books and twenty tons of magazines, newspapers, and phonograph records, without losing one item. With the money saved by Jaycee ingenuity and work, the library could buy $3,000 worth of new books.

Operation Library swept the country. Edmonds wrote hundreds of letters, wrote bulletins and articles for numerous publications, attended library meetings all over the country, and personally contacted each senator and representative on behalf of the Library Services Act. Then he went to the JCI World Congress in Tokyo, and made Operation Library an international project.

All this time, you remember, he was also fighting the long battle for a new library back home. Finally it was over, with Edmonds the victor. He scheduled a big banquet to be held with the ground-breaking ceremony, and, naturally, insisted on making all the arrangements himself. What he did not know was that the national Jaycees were also making arrangements. Their project was called Operation Silence. It was elaborately planned. Yet it was all done in secret, with the motto: "A slip of the lip can ruin our banquet."

And so the banquet began. It started out just fine, with Cecil Edmonds bossing everything. Then, suddenly, out of nowhere appeared three national Jaycee vice-presidents, Bob Cox, Wally Heatwole, and Dixie Lynch, one of whom would be national president the following year. As they came forward, a huge banner was suddenly unfurled in the background. It said, simply, but in mighty big letters,

THANK YOU CECIL

Then, in rapid succession, as his fellow townspeople and Jaycees roared out their cheers, Cecil Edmonds received one honor after the other. He was named Jaycee of the Year, presented with the Distinguished Service Award, made a JCI senator for life. Cecil Edmonds, the Arkansas bulldozer, could only stand helplessly, tears of happiness pouring down his cheeks.

Many Jaycee community projects of national importance have come about through the enthusiasm of one member. Dr. Dan B. Kahle, for example, was largely responsible for the entire Junior Chamber Community Health Program. Dr. Kahle was not a particularly active member in Bloomington, Indiana, where he was a member of the faculty of the Indiana Medical School. But he happened to go to the Atlanta convention, and liked the city. And so, when he went into private practice, Atlanta was the place he chose. He plunged into Junior Chamber activities. After getting a health program going in Atlanta, he became state chairman, helped Jaycees all over Georgia improve the health of their communities.

The American Medical Association invited him to give a paper on the Junior Chamber Health Program. He had hardly finished before representatives of major health organizations came up to congratulate him and offer their services. Dan Kahle doesn't fool around; next thing they knew they were in the Jaycee National Advisory Committee, composed of representatives of the AMA itself, the American Hospital Association, American Dental Association, and the Association of State and Territorial Health Officers.

The Jaycee ten-point health program includes immunization against disease, fluoridation of drinking water, health forums, recreation for mental hospital patients, establishment of a directory of health services, methods of combating accidental poisoning of children, health for handicapped children, staging of a health fair, combating alcoholism, and combating rabies.

It seems incredible, but even this program has met with some opposition. Some people felt Jaycees should stay away from the alcoholism problem, on the premise that only older men are alcoholics. Dr. Kahle was able to show, through facts and figures, that alcoholism frequently attacks men and women of Jaycee age.

Dr. Kahle was completely unprepared for the personal vilification thrown at him as a result of the fluoridation part of the program. Fluoridation of drinking water is, after all, endorsed by the major health organizations, the AMA and American Dental Association in particular, for it attacks the most common disease of civilized man, tooth decay.

Tooth decay affects small children in particular, causing them pain, their parents expense. In many American communities where a beneficent providence has put a small quantity of fluoride into the water supply, tooth decay is reduced as much as two-thirds. Where fluoride doesn't occur naturally, it's a simple matter for man to add it to the water supply.

Strangely, some people oppose this. It's an ironic fact that although the counties surrounding Atlanta put fluoride in their water, Atlanta itself, home of the Junior Chamber National Health chairman, does not.

"We have an island of tooth decay in a sea of fluoridation," Dr. Kahle says ruefully.

Because he wants the children of his community to suffer less pain, Dr. Kahle has been bitterly attacked. People have gone around whispering that "Kahle" is not an American name. He has even been accused of being a pro-Communist!

"Being called names for activity in a worthwhile endeavor is a compliment," Dr. Kahle says. "This is a truly grass-roots campaign. It's people like the Jaycees, fathers of the small children directly concerned, who will carry on and win this fight."

Jaycees are active in the community-health field all over the country. Many Junior Chambers have their own distinctive health projects. Back in Bloomington, for example, where Dr. Kahle had started, the Jaycees conducted a survey which showed that what the city needed most was a new hospital. They set out to sell 5,000 memberships in a Hospital Corporation. They gave it the full Jaycee treatment, with booths manned by Jaycees wearing intern uniforms at plant gates, on street corners, even in stores in rural areas. They put on a house-to-house canvas, appeared before 31 different groups, sold 5,500 memberships in the first two months of the drive, and put over the hospital.

In St. Louis, Crawford A. King, Jr., a personal friend of the famous Dr. Thomas A. Dooley who did such good work in Indo-China, started the Jaycees collecting medicine samples from local doctors. They have actually collected tons of such material.

Delaware Jaycees also collect these samples. In their first year of operation they collected over $50,000 worth of valuable drugs and medical supplies, sent them to areas where they were needed.

One of the strangest Jaycee health activities took place in Provo, Utah, where the Jaycees adopted a men's ward in the state mental hospital. They've done a great deal to help the poor devils who are patients there.

"The entire health field is made to order for the Junior Chamber," Dr. Kahle says. "What better area could young men possibly find in which to serve their community? What area furnishes greater rewards, greater possibilities for leader training than the health of America?"

10,000 Projects

It's amazing, sometimes, what Jaycees choose to take on—and the energy they put into it. At Burlington, Vermont, Ralph Nading Hill, Jr., got terribly excited when he learned that the historic old Lake Champlain side-wheeler *Ticonderoga* was doomed for the scrap heap. Although the Burlington Junior Chamber had just received its charter, Hill goaded his fellow Jaycees into a great crusade—"Save the *Ti!*"

First they raised $10,000 to get the old steamer out of hock. Then they had to have a new dock. The Jay-

cees rounded up forty pontoons, found a whole grove
of elm trees which were felled, trucked to the lake,
and made into pilings. Next the tired old engines had
to be rebuilt. And finally the good old *Ti,* laden with
happy people of this historic section of America,
steamed around the lake, paddle wheel a-sloshing,
whistle a-blowing, bells a-ringing, and Ralph Hill and
the Jaycees happy as kings.

Jaycees have been doing things like this for over
a generation now. Back in 1929, when the movement
was hardly dry behind the ears, the Mobile, Alabama,
Jaycees decided, of all things, to plant flowers. Not just
ordinary flowers, but azaleas. Not just a few azaleas,
but 35 miles of them.

The Jaycees raised funds for the azaleas to be planted
in public places, arranged for nurseries to sell them at
a reasonable price to homeowners. Then the Jaycees
sent three letters to each home owner, visited the difficult ones personally. They saw to it that each of the
thousands of azaleas was planted properly, packed with
peat moss, protected by a small fence, watered regularly
(but not too much, mind you), and carefully weeded.

Today some of these azaleas are thirty feet in di-
ameter, eighteen feet high. They are white, pink, and
red. The Azalea Trail attracts tourists the world over.
"When azaleas bloom," said the National Geographic
magazine, "Mobile is in a crimson blaze, as if a giant
10-mile brush had painted the whole town red."

Well, that was no giant, that was the Mobile Junior
Chamber.

In case your route to the Azalea Trail takes you
through Maryville, Tennessee, and in case you are

waved to the curb by a grim-looking policeman, you might just happen to be in luck. One day a week the Maryville Jaycees select a Tourist of the Day. You'll get free meals, free lodging, movies, bowling, swimming, a tour of the city, flowers, candy, radio interview, picture and write-up in the local paper (sent to your home town paper), and a Jaycee and his wife are your hosts for the evening. While all this is going on, your car is being greased, given an oil change and a tank of gas.

"One time," recalls Dean Stone, past president of the Junior Chamber, "police stopped a man from Atlanta. He was tickled pink. 'What did I win?' he asked. He wasn't so pleased when he found out his prize was a ticket for speeding!"

A Jaycee project which has had truly heart-warming results is North Carolina's Jaycee Prisoner Rehabilitation Program which has aided 700 former prisoners of the state penitentiary in getting a fresh start in the world. Normally two-thirds of all released prisoners wind up in the pen again sooner or later. But of those who have gone through the Jaycee program, the great majority are not only still at home, but are making a real contribution to their communities.

"The state benefits, too," says Jaycee W. R. Henderson, who, as state purchasing officer, should know. "It costs the prison department $900 a year to take care of an inmate. But when that inmate takes his place in society, the state not only saves $900, but gains a wage earner and taxpayer."

This project begins, in each case, months before the prisoner is actually released. Jaycees find him a job, a place to live, attend to all other details necessary to get him started on his own. Sometimes, it's true, the ex-con plays the Junior Chamber for a sucker.

"However," Bill Henderson says, "we have a feeling of genuine satisfaction in knowing that we have helped hundreds of men regain the status of responsible citizens."

Philadelphia Jaycees have also been active in the rehabilitation field. The Jaycee Parole Committee has handled some 500 cases since its formation in the late forties. In many cases, a prisoner is eligible for parole but cannot meet the requirements of a job, a place to stay, and a volunteer counselor. That's when the Jaycee Parole Committee steps in.

Jaycees have often gone far beyond their own city or state limits to help people in trouble. During the days of bloody reprisals against the Freedom Fighters of Hungary, Junior Chambers all over the country welcomed Hungarian refugee families to their cities. Just to prove how impossible it is to please all the people all the time, one Junior Chamber even got itself into hot water by helping a Hungarian family fleeing communism find lodgings and employment.

It happened in Marblehead, Massachusetts. The local Jaycees were quite happy about bringing a Hungarian family to their town. Then one morning they opened the newspaper to read a scathing attack on their project on the grounds they ought to be helping jobless Americans instead of foreigners. The whole town leaped happily into the fray, and it was in the headlines all over Massachusetts. Eventually, of course, the town received the Hungarian family with open arms.

It's amazing how one good act spreads to so many

people and areas. The Jaycees of Clio, Michigan, population 2,077, learned that a Korean student was going to be unable to continue his education through lack of funds. They had to work fast, but by the Bosses' Night banquet all arrangements had been completed.

The student, Charlie Chyung, was inveigled into coming to Clio for the banquet, where the surprise presentation of the scholarship was made. Charlie was speechless with surprise and happiness.

The story by no means ended there. Through Charlie's letters and visits to the Clio Jaycees the whole town has become aware of the problems of the foreign student in America.

"I never be lonely again on my way," wrote Charlie.

One day it was the Clio Jaycees' turn to be surprised. A letter arrived from Charles Chang, president of the Korea Junior Chamber. News of the scholarship had reached Korea, and, through the Korean Jaycees, a whole nation was inspired and encouraged by the thirty-five Jaycees of Clio, Michigan!

To many Junior Chambers these individual local projects are of more importance than the big national programs. Some Jaycee leaders, like Seiji Horiuchi, the Colorado fertilizer salesman who was one of the most personally popular national vice-presidents of all time, have even used local emphasis as a campaign issue.

"When I was president of the Colorado Jaycees," Sage, as he is affectionately known, said bluntly, "I didn't give a damn about Colorado being first in the parade of the states and all that jazz. What I wanted was for every local to do what was best for its own com-

munity. We sent out instructions to every individual
Jaycee in the state, showing how he could find what his
community really needed, really wanted. You'd be
surprised at some of the things we found. In Colorado
Springs, for example, it seemed that although the city
had a wonderful auditorium, it wasn't marked. So the
local Junior Chamber put up signs directing visitors
to it, and gave it a big marquee. Now there's a project
that went over with the people, Dad!"

Paul Bagwell, when he was president, wrote down
an actual list of 10,000 Jaycee projects. Space won't
permit such a list here; instead, here are a few pages of
local activities representative of the projects carried on
each year the world over.

To begin with, many local chapters conduct a survey
of some kind. In Red Lion, Pennsylvania, the Jaycees
set out to learn the reason why young people were leaving town. Reason: not enough industry. So then the
Jaycees set out to find industry and induce it to come
to town.

In Ketchikan, Alaska, the determined and eager Jaycees—150 strong—put in six months of research, came
up with a 64-page, 22,000-word report, with suggestions
for 34 needed community improvement projects.

Why, wondered the Jaycees of Hightstown, New
Jersey, did the voters defeat a referendum for a new
school construction? Why did they turn down a new
playground? The only way to find out was to ask. With
carefully prepared questions, they called one out of
every four families in the phone book. When the results
were in and analyzed, they were amazed at the way the
people ran down their own community. One good

thing: Although the Junior Chamber was less than two years old, many people felt that it was the group doing the most for the community. And so, with at least an understanding of public opinion in Hightstown, the Jaycees set out to change it.

At Jamestown, Rhode Island, the local citizenry seemed in arms about the possibility of an oil refinery coming in and ruining the town as a tourist resort. Everybody talked, but nobody really understood the issues involved or what the people really wanted. The Jaycees took on the job. They interviewed spokesmen for both sides, took written statements, and made hundreds of photographs. They studied naval installations, other refineries, the resort potential of the island, and held public hearings. Finally they announced their findings. The refinery would mean 300 jobs and an additional income of 80 million dollars to the town. That is just exactly what the people wanted, by a tremendous margin.

Of course Jaycees often go much further than a survey. In 1957 little Wewoka, Oklahoma, was hard hit by the decline of the oil business. A manufacturer was interested in setting up in the town, but couldn't afford the move right then. "Start packing," wired the Wewoka Jaycees. "We'll help you."

The Jaycees raised $5,000 for the move. Then they raised $40,000 to put an old building in good repair. The new company moved in and soon had seventy-two local people on its payroll, largest in the community.

The Las Cruces, New Mexico, Jaycees didn't bring in new business; they brought back the old. Local people had begun shopping in El Paso, 44 miles away.

The Jaycees put on several stunts to keep the shoppers home. They assigned each local resident a number, for example, then posted numbers in the back of each local store. If you found your number, you won a prize. After it was all over the Jaycees found they had forgotten to post a number in one merchant's store! They hurried to him, offered to refund the $10 they had gotten from him. The merchant just laughed. Even without the precious number, he had done the largest gross in the history of the store.

It's a far cry from Las Cruces to Princeton, New Jersey, but the Jaycees in that Ivy League college town nevertheless staged a somewhat similar project, leading a movement for conformity in stores and store fronts.

In Pine Bluffs, Wyoming, population 950, the thirty-five Jaycees in the town hold a weekly dance. It brings people to town to spend money, maintains the hall for civic functions—and, one typical year, put $7,085.40 in the Jaycee treasury!

Jaycees love to build parks, even when the only place left is in impossible terrain. In Farmington, New Mexico, for example, all the Jaycees had to work with was a huge gully, thirty feet deep and much wider. For years, it seemed, the Jaycees threw things in that gully, even old automobiles. They prevailed on earth-moving contractors to dump dirt there. And finally it was filled in and grass planted.

"Sometimes," said D. H. Chandler, past local president who went on to state office, "I stand there and look at our lovely park and I just can't believe there'd ever been such an ugly gully there."

The Vero Beach, Florida, Jaycees had nothing but a

semi-tropical jungle to make a park. It took two years, but they finished it, complete with restroom and shower facilities. Naturally the governor appeared at the dedication.

If there is anything worse than a jungle, the Ephrata, Washington, Jaycees would have you know, it's sagebrush. That's what the Jaycees had to clear out, seven acres of it, to put in a new playground.

Although just a year old, the Loogootee, Indiana, Jaycees brought back into service an old park which had been abandoned for years. In Saginaw, Michigan, Jaycees raised $15,000 to buy a parksite, then cleared it themselves—all 80 acres of it. They named the park after the late Elliott A. Imerman, a past president.

Perhaps the granddaddy of all parks is the Jaycee War Memorial playground in Huntington, West Virginia. Started in 1945 in an over-populated area of the city, the playground grew through the years. Today it boasts a wading pool, baseball diamonds, volley ball and basketball courts, and dressing rooms. It has a complete daily recreation program.

In Orange, Virginia, a child's muddy dress not only produced a new playground for the community, but a new president for the Jaycees. When Jaycee Weldon V. Dunn's first-grade daughter kept coming home from the school playground with a muddy dress, he asked the rest of the Jaycees to help him do something about it. First thing he knew he was the new president. Orange got a lovely new playground, part hard-topped, part landscaped grass, with a protective fence all the way around it.

Not too far away, in Woodstock, the Jaycees went

into the school itself, into the dark, gloomy, school-rooms. They painted the dark walls a light pastel shade, installed fluorescent lighting, sanded the dark floor to a natural oak color. They replaced the old black slate boards with green boards, installed venetian blinds and light-colored desks capable of being rotated to catch the light from the windows. One small boy commented, after it was all over: "Gee, it's so much brighter that it's almost fun going to school nowadays." Of course, gloomy school rooms are actually a deterrent to the normal development of American youngsters.

In Colville, Washington, Jaycees cut down several hundred small trees which would otherwise be destroyed, got them out of the forest and to the lumber mill, and raised enough money to put up the 90-foot light poles for the new athletic field.

While the Colville Jaycees were cutting trees, Cheyenne, Wyoming, Jaycees were planting them. Five thousand flowering crab apple trees now grow in Cheyenne, thanks to the Jaycees.

Across the country in Providence, Rhode Island, the Jaycees called on ingenuity. The Starlight Pops Committee found that the only place to hold their concert was in the football stadium. But the acoustics were impossible, nor was it possible to build an acoustical stage. So they took a shell of a standard quonset hut, thirty feet long, cut it down the middle longitudinally, placed the two halves side by side, facing the same way, and had a sixty-foot acoustical shell.

One of the strangest projects was at Wallingford, Connecticut, where the Jaycees brightened and modernized a gloomy old cemetery right in the heart of town.

The number of towns where Jaycees have helped with street signs must run into the hundreds. In many towns, like Chilicothe, Ohio, where Jaycees raised funds for 338 street signs in one year, the signs bear the Jaycee emblem.

There are all sorts of ways of doing it. In Dallastown, Pennsylvania, and Camden, Arkansas, the Jaycees raised the money for the signs and the city council put them up.

In Jacksonville, Illinois, where the council had been discussing the problem for years, the Jaycees took over. They counted corners, ordered 375 signs (the city paid). Next Sunday the Jaycees put in 375 sign posts, and the Sunday after that they attached the signs.

In sprawling La Marque, Texas, with 65 miles of streets, many short and unmarked, the Jaycees put up 224 new concrete markers and renovated, with white paint and red reflector letters, 186 old ones.

Jaycees are particularly good at fitting their projects to the special mood of the town. For years the Jaycees of Hampton County, South Carolina, have been staging the annual watermelon festival, a really big event in this number one watermelon producing area.

Big, blustering Chicago had to do something not only first, but big. They came up with the first Jaycee television series, "You and Your Money," written and produced by Jaycee Bill Watson. Interesting and educational, the program ran for eleven weeks.

Jaycees of Milton-Freewater, Oregon, did the next

best thing. TV reception in that area is poor. A private
concern began building a reflector station on a nearby
mountain, but went broke. The Jaycees raised money,
finished the job and brought television to their community.

The Clarence, New York, Jaycees also stepped into
the entertainment world, promoting youth activity in
music. Its Jaycee Parade of Bands for Teen-agers became the number one New York project.

In Los Angeles, among its scores of projects, the
Junior Chamber stages a real long-hair musicale, the
Chamber Music Festival. At the seventh annual festival,
in 1958, a composition which had not been heard for
three centuries was performed.

More unique projects: In the brand-new and well-
planned city of La Mirada, California, population
50,000, which came with a built-in shopping center,
college, and golf course, Jaycees sponsored the community's opening with a huge open house. In La
Mirada's first year, brand new local and brand new
community, the Jaycees ran thirty-six separate projects.

In Dodge City, Kansas, where Bat Masterson, Wyatt
Earp, and other famous western heroes used to shoot
up Boot Hill regularly, the hill and its little museum
were becoming increasingly dilapidated. The Jaycees
took it over. Now you really have something reminiscent of the Old West to see when you visit Dodge
City.

The Rapides parish Jaycees of Louisiana, in 1946,
took over the dilapidated remains of what had once
been one of the world's most flourishing spas, Hot
Wells. They began with a simple wooden bathhouse.

Since then the state of Louisiana has built a $350,000 central bathhouse, with an additional appropriation of $450,000. It's a huge operation now—but the Jaycees still run it.

In Gettysburg, Pennsylvania, heart of one of America's historical regions, the Jaycees stage the annual antique show, one of the most important in the East.

In Forest City, Iowa, the Jaycees staged a builders and home show. One year a starry-eyed young couple wandered in; they were eloping. The Jaycees set up a wedding ceremony for them complete with flowers, music and vocalist, gifts, a shower of rice, a flower girl, a father to give away the bride, a tape recording of the ceremony, wedding pictures, and a police escort out of town.

If the young couple go to Silver Springs, Maryland, incidentally, they'll find plenty of trustworthy baby sitters, for the Jaycees there conduct a baby-sitter school. Graduates are trained in everything from fire prevention to feeding, clothing, bathing and entertaining the baby.

In Topeka, Kansas, home of the Forbes Air Force Base, Jaycees stage a program to make the airmen of the base welcome in Topeka. What with dances, barbecues, and picnics, special discount rates at movies and concerts, and just plain family hospitality, it's no wonder that servicemen say, "Topeka's the best airmen's town in the world."

In Downer's Grove, Illinois, the Jaycees set out to make another class of people welcome—school teachers. The Jaycees had been active in the school-building program. Now, with the teacher shortage, how were they to get teachers for the new classrooms? First they invited teachers to come see Downer's Grove, and many teachers took them up on it. Jaycees met the visiting teachers, took them on a tour, arranged for overnight hospitality, showed them the town. Next year all classrooms had good teachers.

Many Jaycee chapters have bought rescue wagons for their communities, fitted them with two-way radios, medical kits, even portable iron lungs. One of the finest of these is the Erie, Pennsylvania, rescue wagon, which is almost a moving hospital.

Sometimes trouble happens before the Jaycees could possibly prepare for it. Two days before they received their official charter, the Grand Island, New York, Jaycees had a tragic occasion to help one of their own members. His house burned down, leaving the Jaycee, his wife, and children homeless, without clothing or food. The new chapter went to work immediately, clearing away the rubble and building a rude shelter for the undamaged equipment in the basement. At times as many as fifty Jaycees were on the job. But by nightfall it was complete.

Other Jaycee chapters maintain special police patrols, ready to spring to action in any emergency. One night the special police patrol of Russell, Kansas, was returning after late duty along the flooding Arkansas River, when word came of a flash flood at Hays, 25 miles away. The Jaycees sped to the stricken town. They took over traffic control, joined other rescue groups. One group of five Jaycees made a human chain across a street, down which water was raging shoulder high, to rescue the occupants of several homes.

Speaking of floods, Hyattsville, Maryland, Jaycees found themselves getting increasingly tired of all that water. Seems that the intersection of U.S. Highways 1 and 50, on the doorstep of Washington, D.C., was so frequently flooded that thirty days out of the year traffic had to be detoured around. Even though an adequate flood-control remedy would cost 14 million dollars, the Jaycees went out and fought for it. They won. Now you can drive through Hyattsville in the very worst of weather.

In Forest, Mississippi, the Jaycees found themselves growing increasingly tired of something else—mosquitoes. They staged one of the most complete programs of mosquito extinction in history.

Although Jaycees are men of action, they still have time to administer to the spiritual needs of the community. Remember all the publicity when Phenix City, Alabama, had a national reputation for crime and gambling? After the city chased out the undesirable elements, the Jaycees staged one of the most effective "Come to Church," programs in the nation. Though there was no daily paper or radio station in Phenix City, the Jaycees still managed to inform most of the 23,000 residents of the city that they would be welcome in church that Sunday. Transportation was arranged. Jaycees were present at each of the city's fifty churches. Since then, the ministers of Phenix City say, more and more people have steadily been coming back to church.

Nearly every Junior Chamber sponsors a religious project of one kind or another under its RIAL (Religion in American Life) program. Some of the local chapters have most effective and unusual programs. In Zanesville, Ohio, for example, the Jaycees presented a concert by choirs of all faiths. It was a lovely and moving program with choirs from Protestant and Catholic churches and the Jewish Synagogue pouring forth their voices in praise of Almighty God.

In Cleveland, Ohio, Jaycees arranged services for people who would otherwise never be able to attend. Three separate drive-in theaters were used, one for Catholic, one for Protestant, one for Jewish services. In ambulances, station wagons, and automobiles, the crippled, the aged, the infirm were delivered to the services by the Jaycees. Nurses were in attendance.

For the Jaycees, in performing their service to humanity, do not forget

That faith in God gives meaning and purpose to human life.

9 | *KIDS, KIDS, KIDS*

IT'S 2 A.M. in Dayton, Ohio; the city is asleep, and all is quiet. In a small, cluttered bedroom, a fifteen-year-old boy is sleeping. Suddenly there's a muffled sound. The boy stirs, opens his eyes. He gropes for the alarm clock, wrapped in a sweater and stuffed under a pillow, and cuts it off. Stealthily he gets up, dresses, sneaks out of the house. He walks down the deserted street to a car parked in a driveway. With a key stolen days before he unlocks the car and cuts on the ignition. For an hour he drives aimlessly about the deserted streets of the town. Then he returns the car, goes quietly home, back to bed.

So ends another night in this boy's life. . . .

Sooner or later, of course, the boy—let's call him Ronnie—was caught. Probation officers found him a lonely kid, and no wonder. The boy lived with his sister and mother. His father had moved out entirely, refusing to have anything to do with the family. Ronnie's mother and sister had grown closer and closer together, excluding Ronnie. Shy, unwanted, introverted, Ronnie found his circle of friends growing smaller and smaller. Finally he got to the point where his only pleasure in life was driving around in a stolen car at night, thinking gloatingly, *if the guys could see me now!*

Now what in the world could juvenile court do with Ronnie? Send him home to his parents? His parents weren't interested in him. Send him to reform school? He wasn't that bad.

Yet something had to be done. Fortunately, in Dayton, there was something the authorities could do. They called Fred Stetz, chairman of the juvenile relations committee of the Dayton Jaycees.

Fred took over. He studied the boy's history, read the reports on him, and then he ran down the list of fellow Jaycees who had volunteered for the famous Big Brother Program.

Finally Fred nodded, reached for a phone. Next day, a young, pipe-smoking Jaycee named Bill casually dropped around to see Ronnie. They got in Bill's car and drove around, just chatting. Bill took Ronnie home, introduced him to his wife and kids, showed him the old car he was fixing up and the motorboat he was building. He asked Ronnie no questions, offered him no advice.

Gradually Ronnie became almost a part of the family. He helped with the projects, went on the family picnics. One time, on Ronnie's birthday, Bill arranged a special little surprise party, and Ronnie enjoyed it so much there were tears in his eyes. But, as Ronnie said later, it wasn't so much the extra things Bill did as the fact that he was dependable.

"When Bill says he's going to come by, he comes by," Ronnie explained one day. "My father only lives four blocks away, but he never even bothered to send me a card. But Bill was right there."

Gradually, Ronnie came out of his shell. He developed a few friends among the boys his own age, began speaking up more in class. He began talking seriously about going on to college. It began to look as though Ronnie has a chance for a normal, happy life—thanks to Bill and the Jaycee Big Brother Program.

This program has had wonderful, heartwarming success in Dayton. Here is another boy, for example, a kid with a natural aptitude for mathematics. He fell in with a bunch of tough kids who thought such stuff was sissy. The boy had no parental guidance whatsoever, and kept getting deeper and deeper into trouble. Then a Jaycee Big Brother, an athlete and engineer, stepped in. Before long the two would be tossing a football around one minute, working out a problem in math the next. The Big Brother never had to tell the boy that he could be interested in both sports and mathematics; he was proving it all the time in his actions. Today the boy is on the road to being an engineer himself.

There are dozens of these examples. The interesting thing, Fred Stetz says, is that the big brothers really don't actually do anything. They are just *there*. In many cases the boys have been almost driven into delinquency by neglect, scorn, and mistreatment on the part of the parents. All they need is a friend.

The field of youth welfare is a natural for Jaycees. After all, these forceful, energetic young men were kids themselves not too long ago, and few were Pollyannas, either. They understand these kids' problems.

Sometimes, out of the Jaycee ranks comes that rare individual who, though blessed with so much himself, can find compassion and patience for children with so much less. Take Robert H. Clark, Jr., of Des Moines, Iowa, for instance, a young man on whom fortune smiled. Intense, eager, and splendidly endowed physically, Bob won not three, not four, but *five* varsity football letters at Drake University even though he never weighed more than 150 pounds. (He played for one year before World War II, and four-year-eligibility rules were waived.)

Even though Bob broke his arm, his collarbone, several ribs and his nose, and lost several teeth as a result of football injuries, he still came out ahead. For while he was in the hospital he met a pretty nurse named Mariann Seim. It was a perfect match. They were married on a big television show, with resulting presents, of course.

Mariann kept working and put Bob through law school. Just when she decided she'd rather be a mother than a provider, Bob got his law degree and a good job with the Iowa Power and Light Company. He joined the Jaycees when he was twenty-seven years old and started moving right on up to the top. A young man in a hurry, he ran for state president when still president of the Des Moines local, without going through the intervening offices. "You sure are a nervy bastard," somebody told him at a regional meeting.

But Bob maintained, in his campaign, that ability and enthusiasm would make up for lack of experience. The main duty of the president, he said, is to motivate other officers to do their best work. That, he felt, he could do. So did the other Jaycees. He was elected president.

In the meantime, thanks to Bob's Jaycee work, the company had pulled him out of claims, elevated him to customer-relations work. One day a company executive got him together with Dr. Alfred Sasser, another driving personality. Dr. Sasser, superintendent of the Glenwood State School for the Mentally Retarded and a real crusader, sold Bob on the importance of doing something for these unfortunate children. Out of their conversation at lunch that day grew plans to take some of them on a trip. It would be an incentive to all children; and for those selected, many of whom had been in the hospital since infancy, it would be their only chance ever to go anywhere.

For centuries, mentally retarded children, certainly through no fault of their own, have been the victims of apathy, discrimination, even mistreatment. Here, Bob Clark felt, was an opportunity not only to help Iowa children in particular, but through the attendant publicity all retarded children in general.

Bob's enthusiasm spread through the state. For this one project the Iowa Jaycees raised $4,258.52. Some of the smaller chapters, with as few as 20 men, contributed as much as $150 toward this single project.

Disneyland, near Los Angeles, was chosen as the destination. All details—obtaining permission from parents, transportation for twenty-four kids—were worked out. Chapters en route were contacted, and Jaycees in Cheyenne, Wyoming, Salt Lake City and Anaheim, California, were a great help. The whole project was a thumping success. The kids had a marvelous time. Some received lasting benefits from the trip.

"Here's one of the most amazing results of all," Bob Clark reported after the trip. "One of the kids was not only retarded, but had no family. Thanks to all the publicity, a family related to him learned where he was. They took him out of the institution and brought him in to live with them. Just think, we found a boy a home!"

Chicago Jaycees have also done a great job for retarded children, helping their national association get off the ground with a big fund-raising drive.

Another inspiring Jaycee program got its start in Bakersfield, California, some years ago. One of the members of the Junior Chamber then was John Eaton, who, though a victim of cerebral palsy, with its attendant muscle spasms, jerks, and facial grimaces, had gone through high school and college, gotten a good position.

Like many other sufferers of cerebral palsy, Eaton had been shut in as a child. When he was thirteen he joined the Boy Scouts. The association with normal boys encouraged him to try public school, and from then on he was on the road to a useful life.

With the help of the Bakersfield Jaycees, Eaton organized the world's first scout troop for handicapped children. It was difficult at first to get parents to permit their children to join. Some parents of handicapped children want to protect them unduly, others are ashamed. But Eaton won many parents over. In his first group was a boy with a wooden leg, two boys who had been paralyzed by polio, one with epilepsy, another with hemophilia, as well as the boys with cerebral palsy.

Eaton took the boys on regular outings. One of the places they went was a farm where there was an old mule and a wagon, and these kids, many of whom had never been out of their own home before, got the biggest kick in the world out of riding in the wagon. The problems and difficulties of taking care of the kids, many of whom couldn't feed themselves or go to the bathroom, were insignificant when compared to such happiness.

Can you imagine a boy with cerebral palsy putting together a knot board? Well, Bobby Hoffman did. It took him many months, for frequently, after having spent hours on a tricky knot, his hand would fly off in an involuntary movement and ruin it all. But Bobby finished the board, had his picture taken with it, and it was worth every minute of it.

Several Jaycees have since served as scoutmaster of the troop John Eaton founded. They have all added to the troop. When Harry B. Jones, who was also California state vice-president, was scoutmaster, he heard of a local boy whose parents had never permitted him to leave the house. The kid spent his entire day in a wheelchair with his hands tied down so they wouldn't fly all over the place. Harry finally got the parents to let him take the boy to outings. He never tied the boy's hands down, even though frequently the boy's hand would fly out and crack Harry in the face.

Harry would always turn toward him with mock anger. "Oh, so you want to fight," he'd growl. "Well, I've got a good mind to stop this car and have it out with you right here and now."

And though the poor kid couldn't talk or laugh, he could understand, and he'd scrape his feet and squirm all over with happiness at being treated like a human being.

Texas Jaycees for many years have helped support Camp Sweeney, the famous summer haven for diabetic children. Many parents of diabetic kids never do give insulin shots to their children, and many children have great difficulty doing it themselves. Many can't afford proper care and training. Yet these children must receive insulin daily in order to survive. At Camp Sweeney the kids are taught all they need to know, even how to give themselves urine tests.

Even more important, in one sense, they can see other diabetic children running and playing, and realize that they, too, can lead a normal life. The kids go to camp frightened, shy, and feeling put upon; they come back happy boys and girls.

Jaycees all over the country are great at this sort of thing. Can you imagine 850 crippled children on one boat trip? The Washington, D.C., Jaycees put on such a junket every year—a cruise down the lovely Potomac to Mount Vernon, home of George Washington.

The Kansas City Jaycees formed Our House Foundation to build a $40,000 children's recreation center. Bangor, Maine, Jaycees raised money for the local school for retarded children. It took the Jackson, Mississippi, Jaycees thirteen years to do it, but when they finished it was worth it—a thirty-five-bed unit, so modern it doesn't even look like a hospital, entirely for children. Cost: $50,000, one of the largest Jaycee donations on record.

In Oklahoma City, Jaycees show up in the Oklahoma Crippled Children's hospital twice a week with games, prizes, movies, refreshments.

Social workers have long known the sad fact that only in fairly large communities do crippled and handicapped children get adequate attention. Since World War II, as Jaycee chapters have spread into smaller communities, this is becoming more and more a thing of the past. Take Mountain City, Tennessee, population 1,390. Its Junior Chamber has close to 100 members who keep busy on scores of projects. One of these is to drive crippled children and their mothers to the nearest clinic, 42 miles away over mountain roads. Among the many children thankful to the Jaycees are a grade-school child who learned to walk and a boy who, after losing his hand in an accident, was provided with an artificial hand.

3,700 Santa Clauses

All Jaycee children's activities seem to reach fever pitch at Christmas time. In big towns and little, Jaycees just go crazy at Christmas. In big, blasé New York City, the junior executives and young professional men of the Young Men's Board of Trade put on a project which proves the goodness of children. The Jaycees round up hundreds of orphans and poor kids, give them several dollars each and turn them loose in Gimbels department store—open on Sunday just for this event—to buy presents. And the most heartwarming thing of all is the number of things the kids buy not for themselves but for others.

The Chicago Jaycees—fifth chapter in the nation—do the same thing, taking hundreds of kids to several big stores.

In Buffalo, New York, the Jaycees' eyes smarted when one of the underprivileged kids to whom they had given five dollars to spend asked if he could make a telephone call. He'd heard about phones but had never used one.

Other big chapters, like Dallas, Atlanta, Phoenix, have huge Christmas programs that make life worth living for thousands of kids, bring that great inner warmth of satisfaction to the hundreds of Jaycees who make it all possible. Whether in Atlanta, where Jaycees raise over $60,000 for Christmas in *one day,* or in little Atlantic, Iowa, where the Jaycees had enough money left over from the shopping tour to buy the children's home two bicycles, a tricycle and an outdoor grill, this warmth of heart is its own reward.

Here are just a few of the many unusual Christmas projects. The Las Vegas Jaycees brought Santa Claus to kids and grown-ups alike in the Havasupai Indian Reservation in the lower recesses of the Grand Canyon, the most remote and primitive spot in the United States. One party of Jaycees rode into the canyon over tortuous trails the night before, while the rest arranged to deliver the Christmas presents in the only possible way, by parachute! Next day the planes appeared over the canyon, and the chutes came down. The aerial display, plus the awareness that somebody cared, was appreciated by the Indians almost as much as the presents and supplies in the chutes.

In Roanoke, Virginia, the Jaycees had to do something in a hurry. A destitute Austrian family moved into town in early December, and the Jaycees learned at the last minute that in Austria presents are given on St. Nicholas's Day, December 6. The Christmas committee was just getting started, but they speeded up operations for this family. Everything went off well, with children buying their parents presents as well as vice versa (cheese for Papa, chocolates for Mama).

The Jaycees provided the family with another Christmas celebration on Christmas day, to get them in the habit for next year.

Jaycees also arranged to answer mail addressed to Santa Claus, man special telephones to take orders from the kids. Christmas projects can take on the aspects of big business. In Austin, Texas, for example, Jaycees collected 23,000 toys. Where in the world will you store 23,000 toys, much less fix them up and deliver them?

The national office sends out kits listing Christmas projects and how to stage them. Other materials benefiting youth are also available. Each year Jaycees all over the nation buy hundreds of thousands of leaflets called "Beware of Strangers" for two cents each and distribute them to schools. The strange thing is that, although Jaycees contribute thousands on thousands of dollars each year to this project, nobody really knows for sure whether the program actually does any good.

"If it saves just one child from embarrassment or

worse at the hands of a sexual deviate," a Jaycee staffer says, "it's worth every penny of it."

The national office also distributes clever little doll sets, which children cut out and color. They subtly but surely get over a message of home and traffic safety.

One of the big, national, heavily publicized projects is the famous Safe Driving Teen-age Road-e-o. This project is carried on in thousands of communities, with the cosponsorship of the Liberty Mutual Insurance Company, American Trucking Association, Inc., the Chrysler Corporation, and the Pure Oil Company.

Anywhere from one to thousands of kids of driving age participate on the local level. They take written tests, then drive an automobile through an extremely difficult series of tests. Here's a sample: Place two tennis balls exactly 11½ inches apart. A few feet farther, in a straight line, put down two more. Then two more, and so on, for 120 feet. Now try to drive your car with the left tires going between these tennis balls for the full distance without touching a single ball. Think you can do it? Road-e-o winners can, and do.

The boys—and sometimes girls—who win first and second place on a local level go to the state contest, where competition is tougher. Two winners from each state go to Washington for the national contest, all expenses paid. For five days, when they're not competing, they have the run of the capital, go behind the scenes, meet prominent people. And the three national winners, in addition to having the time of their young lives, receive cash scholarships of $2,000, $1,500 and $1,000 respectively.

The 1958 winner, Edward M. Smith of Silver

Springs, Maryland, might have been considered, a couple of years before, a dark horse. Ed had had his license for only a few months when he was arrested for speeding. He had to go to special driving school three Friday nights—date nights, too—in a row.

After that Ed set out to be a good driver, not a fast driver. That year—he was sixteen—he was runner-up in his local competition, seventh place in the state. The next year he was first place all the way through.

"The $2,000 scholarship is going a long way at the University of Maryland, where I'm taking an engineering course," Ed said later. "But it was a big thing, too, meeting all those guys from all over the country, finding out how much in common I had with the fellows from big and small towns alike. And I think, also, I've helped the older people in my home town realize that not all teen-agers are hot rodders. I've spoken before several organizations, and I think I've convinced them that many kids like myself are really serious."

Many Jaycee chapters go into the corrective aspects of traffic safety. In Fort Wayne and Muncie, Indiana, for example, Jaycees maintain schools for traffic law violators. In Muncie, Jaycees first worked under the supervision of traffic and safety officials. But as they proved their worth, they took over the whole thing themselves. Within one year the number of "pupils" in the school was reduced from as many as forty at a time to less than half of that.

Another national project is the Young Adult Placement Program. Chattanooga, Tennessee, Jaycees have done a particularly fine job in this field. They began by helping delinquent kids get jobs, for these kids needed the jobs the most, had the most difficulty in finding them. They also lined up jobs for wards of the juvenile court.

If the program worked for juvenile delinquents, why wouldn't it help average kids too? Or even mentally retarded kids? Again the Jaycees went all out. In two weeks 550 youths came in for interviewing and counseling. Then it turned out that there weren't enough jobs. In the summer of 1958 adults were having trouble finding jobs. So Robert A. Elmore, chairman of the Youth Welfare Committee, set up odd-job centers at the thirty-seven city recreation parks. Many kids were able to pick up a few hours work, at least.

Such a program turns up all kinds of things. Two twin brothers, deserted by their mother, were found by police huddling in a boxcar, living on overripe fruit. The youth program committee found them jobs, got them started toward a decent life. One teen-ager got so wrapped up in the Youth Employment program that when he got out of school he set up his own Youth Employment Service.

The proof of the pudding really arrived when Jaycees found it necessary to set up a "Back to School" program in the fall to get the kids out of those jobs, back to school!

Most Jaycee locals have a continuous year-round program of Youth Welfare activities, compete for national recognition. In 1958 the Hagerstown, Indiana, Junior Chamber took first place in this field for towns under 5,000 (actual population: 1,694). Would you like to know what they did? Well, just the bare outline of their activities covers three single-spaced pages, but here are the high spots of some of their programs.

For years the high school seniors had been going off to Cincinnati, even Chicago, for an all-night junket following graduation exercises. The parents would go crazy with worry, but none would be the first to try to stop it. The Jaycees got the other service clubs together, and arranged for an all-night program right there in Hagerstown. The Jaycees themselves agreed to take the most important time, after the graduating exercises until one or two o'clock in the morning. They arranged a special movie, a first-run film. The graduates would drive up in the family car, usually in couples, get out in front of the theatre and some eager Jaycee would drive the car off and park it. Of course, every year, it pours down rain at this stage. After the movie came a snack, then a dance at the country club. Around 7 or 8 A.M. came breakfast and then they let the exhausted kids go home.

Another project was the Boy Scout Explorers' fund-raising car wash. The boys were willing to work, but not old enough to drive. The Jaycees picked up and delivered the cars, and the Explorers did an excellent job on them. They raised $600.

Then they put on the Jaycee relays. The track coach, Bruce Hamman, also a Jaycee, was tired of seeing his boys run their hearts out in a vacuum, so to speak. The Jaycees promised to get a crowd out to a meet, and, hearing that, other schools in the area broke into their already-full schedules and sent full teams. Over 100 boys participated as a big crowd cheered them on. A

Hagerstown boy raised the pole-vault school record one-quarter of an inch and was the hero of the meet.

The high school had had a football team for only three years. The team had yet to win a game. But every year the Jaycees put on a big banquet, and presented awards to just about everybody who went out for the team. Playing on a losing team is hardly fun, but the Jaycees helped a little bit.

The most dangerous project in Hagerstown is the Easter egg hunt. Some years the chairman of the hunt is a young Jaycee who has not seen one before. He always stands in front of the line of kids when he blows the whistle starting the hunt. A moment later, he disappears, under a swarm of children.

In the first year of the hunt, when there was a cash prize, mothers were permitted to accompany their smaller children. One mother nearly jerked her child's arm out of its socket as she dragged him around grabbing up eggs. When a member of the Jaycee committee mildly protested, she started to hit him with the closest weapon handy, the child.

The first year Jaycees and their wives boiled and dyed fifty dozen eggs in one member's kitchen. After the hunt was over you could find your way back to town by the trail of smashed hard-boiled eggs. After the kids had eaten one or two, they began throwing them. A sulphuric smell hung over the town for weeks. Today they use candy eggs, ninety dozen of them, a nickel apiece. Nor do they give prizes any more. A bunch of kids would get together, pool all the eggs and win first prize, then pool them all over again to win second, and so down the line. Sometimes kids are smarter than Jaycees.

There can be no finer way to wind up this chapter on Jaycee youth projects than with the new national project, My True Security.

For years the Junior Chamber had conducted a speaking contest for high school students called Voice of Democracy. It was a good program and got excellent results. But during those years, a former Jaycee national president, H. Bruce Palmer, now president of the Mutual Benefit Life Insurance Company of Newark, had been worrying about the use of the word "security" in American life. Palmer felt more and more that the word was beginning to take on the improper meaning that somebody else is going to take care of you.

Real security, true security, Palmer felt, could be broken down into three parts: First, security in social relationships; that is, acceptance by the people in the community in return for participation in community affairs. Second, business security, in which one looks not to a benevolent corporation or government for protection, but to one's own self for the capacity and energy to produce. Third, financial security, which is more than mere governmental social security, but rather the rewards which redound to the individual in exchange for his planning, working, and contributing toward his own future.

Palmer wrote several large companies for their views on security. Fully 85 per cent of the responses from management said their major administrative problem was the unwillingness of subordinate employees to assume responsibility. These employees seemed content to ride along doing their assigned duties forever. Top management, however, constantly seeks the men willing to assume responsibility, the man who will manage tomorrow. How can you change this situation? "The only way is through the fertile mind of youth," Palmer said. "If you give today's kids an opportunity to study and determine their own basic philosophy of security, we will then be developing a whole new generation of people capable of thinking for themselves, eager to take responsibility, and desirous of looking within themselves for their own security."

And so My True Security was born. All over the nation high school seniors began preparing their scripts, and they naturally looked down deeper in themselves. There were state winners and national winners. But the true worth of the program lies in the aggregate, what all the participants discovered about themselves, rather than in what the top winners said so well.

Take, for example, what Lynn England from South High School in Salt Lake City learned about himself. Lynn placed second in the regional contest, in which students from six high schools participated. He finished sixth in the state contest. But though that's as far as Lynn went in the contest, he has every intention of getting farther in the contest of life.

"I never really thought much about myself, what I was going to do or why, until I got into this contest," Lynn said. "But the more I thought, the more I came to realize that my only true security is me. It's what I do for myself that is going to mean my real happiness in life. Before this contest I wasn't sure about going to college, because I knew I'd have to work my way through. Now I've decided that it's worth it if I have to crawl through on my hands and knees. Funny thing is, although now I've got a lot more work to look forward to, I'm a lot happier that way—and I owe it all to the Jaycees."

10 JUNIOR CHAMBER, COLLEGE OF LEADERSHIP

NO MATTER HOW MANY solid accomplishments the Jaycees have made, at home and around the world, no
matter how many tears of joy they have brought to
children everywhere, the cold hard fact remains: All
this is secondary.

For the primary function of the Junior Chamber of
Commerce the world over is leadership training. It is
on this one objective that the Junior Chamber stands
or falls.

Since its founding in 1920, the Junior Chamber in
the United States alone has turned out over 32,000
officers and directors, experienced executives eager to
serve community and country. How many of this number have reached the top echelon of local, state, and
national leadership defies an accurate count. In government alone, from the Vice President of the United
States, Richard M. Nixon, on down through senators,
congressmen, federal government executives, governors
and state legislators, justices, judges and district attor-
neys, mayors and councilmen ... these alone would
add up into the thousands. How many millionaires,
how many corporation presidents and directors, how
many of the names you read in the big national magazines are or have been Jaycees? Finally, to get down

to a really astronomical figure, how many presidents and directors of local Senior Chambers of Commerce have come out of Jaycee ranks? It would take a Univac to figure it out.

For the Junior Chamber is the answer to the question young men have asked since the dawn of history. Let's put it in the words of J.R. "Pat" Gorman, a prominent Washington attorney and the only national vice-president ever elected from the nation's capital.

Pat was a young fellow just out of Notre Dame and Georgetown Law School when he was interviewed by a national trade association looking for a Washington representative. Everything went fine until he was asked what previous experience he had along these lines. That ended the interview, because Pat had *no* experience.

Out on the street Pat raised his eyes heavenward, and, in silent anguish, asked, "If you can't get a job without experience, and you can't get experience without a job, *then what in the world are you going to do?*"

Not long after that Pat answered his own question. He joined the Junior Chamber of Commerce. He worked on Jaycee committees, was chairman of Jaycee committees, learned to handle people, learned to delegate authority. He was asked to serve in other community organizations; as chairman of the speakers bureau for the Community Chest, he found himself, before he was thirty, sitting at the head table with the biggest people in the nation's capital. And in two years he went back to the trade association.

"Now I've got experience," he said—and landed the account.

The Junior Chamber doesn't exactly throw a new member in water over his head and leave him to sink or swim. But it does, frequently, throw him in first, teach him to swim second. Sometimes a young Jaycee like Edward F. Selleck finds himself out in deep water, trying to swim and read an instruction book at the same time.

Ed was one of the organizers of the Amherst Township Junior Chamber in New York. At the organization meeting he was elected second vice-president. Within six months both the president and first vice-president had left town, and Ed, then twenty-six, found himself handling all three jobs.

In his zeal to get things done, Ed frequently got out and did the work of the committee rather than supervising and encouraging its chairman and members. "Every committee had an extra member and a co-chairman," Ed recalled recently. "Me."

On the first big fund-raising project, selling Christmas trees, it was Selleck who painted the signs, Selleck who rented the vacant lot, Selleck who bought the lights and rigged them up, Selleck who met the truck bringing in the trees, and, finally, he was out there helping sell them too.

By the time the project was over and Ed was a whipped-down wreck, he had learned the advantages of delegating authority.

But all this time he was having more and more success with the more difficult and important administrative duties. For he was conscientiously studying the excellent, well-written, and complete operations manuals the national office furnishes all officers and directors from the local level on up. He was mastering the organization of the local Junior Chamber. He was learning the duties of the officers, the executive committee, the board of directors, the committee chairmen, and, more important, the flow of command. With these manuals, he had the experience of thousands of other Jaycee local presidents right at his fingertips. By following its suggestions he could get his local organized along the best lines commensurate with its membership, he could run a good meeting, he could advise his officers on what records to keep. Before him was solid advice on myriads of details, from maintaining membership to a reminder to thank everybody who helped to put a project over.

After this baptism of fire, and with his wife Nancy behind him all the way, Ed moved right on up the ladder to state president and national vice-president. Six years after it all began he was candidate for president. And all the time he was rocketing along in his career in sales.

It is pretty clear that the Junior Chamber offers its members a chance to gain experience—but what *is* experience? How do you spell it out? One day Harold J. Salfen, a former national vice-president, gave a concrete example of just exactly what he had learned.

Salfen and another young man went to work as ticket agents for Delta Airlines in Atlanta about the same time. A company-sponsored Jaycee dropped out about that time, and somebody looked around, spotted Salfen, and told him to hurry over to the Jaycee luncheon. At his first meeting Hal was so flustered that he introduced himself as, "I'm Delta Airlines representing Hal Salfen."

Hal fought his way up through the rough-and-tough,

give-and-take discussions in committee meetings and executive meetings. Jaycees, incidentally, can argue for hours about anything. And out of this, he gained conference know-how. Translated to the business world, let's say that Hal and other department heads are called in by the big boss to determine a program of action.

"Here's the way you do it," Hal said. "First you say a few words, then sit back and listen. The next guy takes over. He hasn't been through the Jaycee mill, and he's scared and ill at ease. He's got a couple of good suggestions but he mutters and mumbles and they don't get over. The next guy has a good point too, but he's trying to impress the boss and he talks too much. The next guy has never been hooted at by a bunch of Jaycees and he rambles all over the place. So now you quietly get the floor again. You take the good ideas which these guys thought up but couldn't present, organize them, throw away the chaff, and lay them all out in one cohesive whole. That's the program that's adopted. The boss takes you aside afterwards, buys you a drink and congratulates you on it."

In his early thirties Salfen became general sales manager for Delta Airlines. What about that other young man, the one who came to work at the same time? Still a salesman.

This is one of the reasons companies sponsor membership for young employees. Rodney C. Linton, when president of the Detroit Junior Board of Commerce, writing in the Detroit Jaycees' excellent slick-paper journal, expressed it this way:

"Any company, as a progressive organization, is constantly aware of the need to develop in its young men those qualities of leadership, experience and vision they will need as they move to positions of increased responsibility. These are not qualities which can be obtained or developed overnight, and often times normal job opportunities do not permit such experience to the extent that good business managers might desire."

In Los Angeles some of the companies which support members in the Junior Chamber are the Richfield Oil Company, Union Oil Company, General Petroleum Company, Standard Oil, Title Insurance Company, Grand Title Insurance Company, California Gas Company, Edison Company, nearly all the savings and loan companies, the major newspapers and banks. These companies not only pay the members' dues, they make periodic checks with the executive secretary to find out how their employees are doing. If they aren't pulling their own weight, showing progress, the companies yank them out, send somebody else.

In the Los Angeles Junior Chamber, which is a real junior-executive operation, by the time a man works his way up to be president he may well be a $25,000-a-year man with his company. As he will by tradition devote half his day to Junior Chamber activities, half to business, his company is therefore putting up about $12,500 a year for the young executive's experience.

Although a very few big-city Junior Chambers want applicants from junior executive ranks only, most locals are wide open to any man aged twenty-one to thirty-six, even if his job is pumping out cesspools.

That, by coincidence, happened to be just exactly what Fred Rathbun of Phoenix, Arizona, did for a living—he pumped out cesspools. One day he pumped out a cesspool belonging to a Jaycee member, who invited him to a Jaycee meeting sometime—after he'd taken a shower.

Fred did, joined, became an active Jaycee. One time it was necessary for him, as chairman of some project, to meet with the mayor of the town. An emergency came up on a job and Rathbun couldn't get away in time to change clothes. He went straight to the meeting, shook hands with the mayor and the two got the business done smoothly, without batting an eye.

Rathbun went on to stage a successful campaign for the board of directors of the Phoenix Junior Chamber (such a campaign costs a candidate at least $500) and went into business for himself.

At the state and national level, Jaycee leaders rub elbows with officials of national prominence. Training is the same, but broader. Robert D. Ladd, one of the Junior Chamber's most capable executive vice-presidents, once observed that exposure to nationally prominent people provides top-level Jaycees with an opportunity to learn from them in general, rather than direct contacts for positions.

Ladd himself, on leaving the Junior Chamber, became Senator Nixon's executive secretary, then Washington consultant for companies in the technical and scientific fields. Roland T. Tibbetts, executive vice-president from 1956 through 1958, also moved into a high-echelon position in Washington.

Tibbetts, incidentally, was living proof of the Jaycee emphasis on ability over everything else, even internal politics. Harvard Business School graduate, Hartford junior bank executive, Roland was one of the leaders

in the excellent campaign which almost won Edwin
H. May, Jr., the national presidency, did win him a
seat in Congress. Hugh McKenna, who won out over
May, didn't have to look far for an executive vice-
president. Roland Tibbetts, Hugh thought with a sigh
of relief, had proven his ability almost *too* well. And
so Hugh got his opponent's campaign manager in as
his administrative assistant. The entire Junior Chamber benefited, for Roland brought in several administrative improvements.

His successor, Ben Swanson, has his own ideas of
leadership training—hard work. Ben, son of a Swedish
immigrant sawmill worker in Tacoma, Washington,
and a sawmill worker himself in summer vacations,
worked his way through college. Through a friend, he
heard of an opening as accountant at national Jaycee
headquarters halfway across the nation. Ben moved in,
found his predecessor long gone and the books in hopeless condition. He had to teach himself the ropes and
bring things up to date all at the same time. For months
Ben worked every night, every weekend. He didn't
whine, he didn't moan. He just got the job done.

And not long after, when the top administrative job
in the nation opened up, Ben Swanson got it. His
secret? Ability, period.

"Any other young man in the United States could
have gotten this job," Ben said. "All he had to do was
work a little harder, show a little more ability, than I
did."

Many times the Junior Chamber has demanded that
its leaders show this ability under extremely trying
conditions. H. Bruce Palmer, wartime national presi-

dent whose appearances at public functions in company with state and national dignitaries were made all the more hectic because of travel conditions, has often said that after his year of service he'd never again be afraid to do anything. Not too many years later he was put to the test.

Palmer was then general agent for the Mutual Benefit Life Insurance Company in his hometown of Flint, Michigan. The company underwent reorganization and all general agents were summoned to appear at the home office in Newark. The new chairman of the board, W. Paul Stillman, asked Palmer to become his personal assistant.

Palmer thought it over. Back at Flint he had a high income and a secure future. In Newark he'd take a 75 per cent cut in income, and be faced with an enormous challenge. He didn't hesitate—he took the job. A few years later, in his early forties, he became the president of one of the country's twelve largest insurance companies.

Though leadership pays great rewards, it also exacts a toll. One of the Jaycees most valuable and thought-provoking manuals is *The Price of Leadership,* product of Ed Merdes, the Alaska dynamo, and Dr. Fred E. Fiedler, Vienna-born psychologist. The manual gives excellent tips on leadership, but it also points out some of the sacrifices necessary.

For one thing, the most effective leaders are not always the most popular individuals. Leadership requires a certain amount of ruthlessness. "If a job needs to be done, the leader must be ready to fire his own grandmother if she can't do it."

Nor can a leader continue to be just one of the gang. Some former Jaycee presidents have proved themselves capable of paying the price. In Bruce Palmer's first two years with Mutual Benefit, he retired forty-five of sixty-five general agents. A period of phenomenal growth ensued.

Another former president, General Condon, at the personal appeal of the mayor of New York, assumed command of Civil Defense of the New York metropolitan area. The General was horrified to find the organization filled with hundreds of hangers-on, and consequently unprepared for any emergency whatsoever. The General frankly admitted, later, that it was his lessons of leadership learned as a young man in the Jaycee movement which gave him the strength to slash hundreds of employees from the payroll.

At least one Jaycee proved himself capable of necessary ruthlessness on the state Jaycee level. Strangely, this young man, one of the Junior Chambers' strongest, most effective leaders, was almost refused membership. When the young men of Watsonville, California, started organizing their Junior Chamber, there was heavy debate on whether A. M. "Red" Ghahremani should be accepted in the group. Red, whose fiery thatch made his nickname obvious, had come from his native Persia only a few years before. He had gotten two degrees in California universities, but his accent made it almost impossible to understand him.

Red squeezed in, however, and, as he says with a grin, "I've been talking ever since." He talked his way right on up to the top; in 1958 he was elected president of the California Jaycees. Then he began laying about him with an ax. When he got through he had cut the total number of California chapters from 217 to 209, membership from 10,600 to 8,200. But the pruning was effective, for soon the number of chapters was back to 219, membership over 11,000.

From the chairmanship of the most insignificant committee of the smallest local to the national presidency, Jaycee leadership poses its difficulties. Any Jaycee can tell you of young men who have quietly quit and gone back to their daytime job and nighttime TV watching. And there's the true story of a young Dutchman who escaped the Nazis during World War II, made his way to England, joined the Royal Air Force, and shot down many German planes in personal combat. He came to the United States after the war, joined the Junior Chamber, and reached a high state office. And then, under the responsibilities of his new duties he had a complete mental breakdown.

Mearns T. Gates, the popular public school superintendent from Pomeroy, Washington, who was national president in 1944–45, became ill towards the end of his term and had to retire. The burden was passed on to Henry Kearns, who took over the reins. Kearns was home just exactly thirteen nights in the thirteen months he served. He sold his business when he became president and spent $20,000 of his own money during his term.

Allen Whitfield, president in 1935–36, who has known every national president, points out an ironic situation which occurs in the case of many former Jaycee officers.

"Young men are hard and cold in sizing up a member of their own generation," Whitfield said. "Young men judge other men not by how much money they have, not who their father or their wife's father was, but by what kind of a guy is *he,* what can *he* do. In a young men's organization, the young man who delivers the goods gets the job. But time and again I've seen men who got to the top in their local Junior Chamber try to repeat their success in an older group or business, and get set back hard for their pains. They lose out to the man who married the boss's daughter, or a member of one of the old families of the town or a fellow with a more popular national origin or religion. It might even be someone of utter incompetence whom the older fellows just happen to feel sorry for. Sometimes the ex-Jaycee just doesn't understand it, and is bitterly hurt."

One of the great human stories of the Junior Chamber, bittersweet yet inspiring, deals with the young man who accepted so completely its lofty ideals and glorious hopes that he couldn't compromise with anything less. That, in a sense, is what happened to Horace E. Henderson, president in 1952–53.

"Hunk" Henderson came riding out of Virginia like a fair-haired knight on a white charger. Boyish, enthusiastic, with a brilliant mind and a glowing personality, Hunk had been looking for something like the Junior Chamber long before he found it. As a young officer in World War II, he had fought his way from Normandy to Berlin. He saw death, suffering, and the atrocities of the concentration camps.

Why must such things be? he asked himself. *What can I do to prevent this from ever happening again?*

Foot-loose after the war, looking for something but not knowing what it was, Hunk wandered to Florida. And there, in Orlando, he found it, found it at a Jaycee luncheon. There was a good program at that luncheon, as is always the case in Orlando's large and powerful Junior Chamber, and afterwards several constructive activities were discussed. Hunk was fascinated and enthralled by the way the 300 young men at the meeting threw themselves into this movement. This, Hunk knew, was for him.

He went back home to Williamsburg, Virginia, into the real estate and insurance business, and organized a Junior Chamber. He went right on up to the top. You couldn't have held him down with an anchor off a battleship. In the shortest election that the national Junior Chamber has ever had, he was elected president on the first ballot. Nor was he up against any patsy, either. For the man he defeated, Douglas L. Hoge of Cincinnati, was later elected president of Junior Chamber International!

As national president, Hunk covered the nation and the world like a grinning blond whirlwind. On his way back from the JCI world conference in Melbourne, he had a couple of hours in New Delhi between planes. He promptly organized a Junior Chamber, the first in India. The first man he talked to was Parshotam L. Mehta, who later became national president.

At the close of his year, the Minneapolis convention was addressed for the first time by a President of the United States, the newly elected Dwight D. Eisenhower. President Eisenhower was standing in the wings, ready to go on, when he heard a voice roar over the public address system: "And now, I give you the greatest president we have ever had. . . ." Eisenhower started forward, but hands reached out and dragged him back as the voice went on . . . *"Horace E. "Hunk" Henderson!"*

After the program Hunk went up to the President earnestly. "Mr. President," he said, "we have a quarter of a million members in this organization. What can we do?"

President Eisenhower looked at him closely for a moment. Then he said, "Mr. Henderson, the best solution to the problem that faces our nation today lies in the development of enlightened leadership."

Those words stuck with Henderson. He translated them into the entire world. "The great masses of people all over the world," he explained, "with centuries, even thousands of years of accumulated culture behind them, can hardly be changed overnight, either for better or for worse. But if we could reach the *leadership* of those people, they can be changed in half an hour, and for the better!"

And so Hunk Henderson went out into the world, to change the thinking of its leaders. He spent a year traveling the globe, studying, observing, organizing. In that year he founded new chapters in twenty countries —Norway, Finland, Iran, Pakistan, Burma—and reorganized chapters in several South American countries. Eager, enthusiastic and earnest, wherever he went he found people to listen to him, people to act on his proposals. Here was a young man actually in the act of changing the world!

In some areas, where he found the great majority of

people living under difficult and oppressive conditions, Hunk was shocked and saddened. But the greatest shock of all was when he came home, settled down, and then discovered that many of the people in his own home were living under a form of political oppression.

"I've never realized it before," he said later, "but now I saw that in my own home town was the very minimum opportunity for the citizen to participate in government. The political atmosphere was stifling! I found complete control of electoral machinery by one political party. I saw people stand in line two hours to vote, then, when they could not produce their poll tax receipts, were sent back home to get them. You figure how many of those people returned to stand in line for two more hours. Government came down from the top. Our welfare record, educational facilities were shockingly poor. For all efforts were devoted entirely to supporting the status quo."

Hunk set out to change that situation. He had been president of the Junior Chamber of Commerce, he had toured the world, and now he ran for Congress. Because the established machine bore the Democratic party label, he ran as a Republican. And although Hunk Henderson could bring about great changes in India, he could not get the people of Tidewater, Virginia to elect a Republican. Hunk missed election by only 2 per cent of the vote, but he missed.

Then he ran for lieutenant governor of the state, on a combination Republican-Reform ticket. The state was in a period of great unrest over the issue of integration of public schools, and the Republican ticket was charged with being pro-integration. Every candidate but Henderson denied the charge vehemently. But Hunk Henderson, although he had been raised in the South, although he had supported the Dixiecrat ticket in 1948, could no longer follow the segregation-at-any-price line. He alone spoke out fearlessly and publicly against abolishing public schools rather than have any amount of integration. The ticket took a shellacking at the polls. Henderson was finished in Virginia. He wasn't yet forty.

But he still believed he could serve, if not at home, then in the world. He took his program to another ex-Jaycee, Vice-president Nixon. Henderson proposed a people-to-people program, constructive and positive.

"Let's call it a citizenship assistance program," he said. "We'd provide technical self-help and know how in the field of citizenship activities just as we are already doing in technical assistance fields. We'd stimulate participation of civic groups organized on an international basis, like JCI. We'd develop citizens, leaders with enthusiasm and know how, people on our side!"

"It sounds good," the Vice-president said, "write it down and let's see what we can do with it."

Hunk wrote it down, all right—on a typewriter in Nixon's office, then and there. Before long, Hunk Henderson found himself Deputy Assistant Secretary of State, charged with carrying out his own program.

Between the time Hunk Henderson stepped down from the Jaycee presidency with the cheers of his fellow Jaycees ringing in his ears and the time he took up his new portfolio in the Department of State, he had given up his business and lost any hope of successful political

activity in his home state in the foreseeable future. He
had lost his domestic happiness, for his wife had tired
of his constant traveling and secured a legal separation.

And here, in the life of Hunk Henderson, as he goes
home to a lonely bachelor apartment at the end of the
day, is another price of leadership. He was born to
success, success in almost anything except running for
office as a moderate in segregationist Virginia, anything except trying to be a husband and father while
half a world away. But a leader can't step back, a leader
must go forward. A leader pays the price.

II | *THE HANDS OF YOUTH AND ACTION*

ONCE A YEAR, in an inspiring and significant ceremony, the United States Junior Chamber of Commerce makes its annual presentation of awards to America's Ten Outstanding Young Men, and in so doing proudly displays the whole theme of the Jaycee movement for all the world to see. For the ten young men who annually are so honored—there have been well over 200 of them —are not only symbols of what young men of America can do, but also, in many cases, portend even greater leaders of the future.

As national president Charles E. Shearer, Jr., said, in presenting the awards to the ten outstanding young men of 1957: "Because of the accomplishments of these young men, this great land of ours will continue to grow and prosper. Because of their dedication to their fields of endeavor, our lives become richer, for they have achieved heights of accomplishments that benefit all peoples. In this era of world unrest these young men stand out as leaders who can furnish all young people with goals that will serve as inspiration to them."

Over the years these young men have come from many fields of endeavor. Some, whose accomplishments were performed in areas not generally rewarded by public acclaim, have been brought out of their quiet laboratories or their local communities to stand in the national spotlight as an inspiration to all other young men who serve mankind in like fields. Others have already achieved national prominence, but the Junior Chamber's recognition of their accomplishments tells the world that these men are *young* men.

The father of the TOYM program was Durward Howes, national Jaycee president in 1930–31, a prominent Los Angeles jeweler who also designed the Jaycee shield. For several years outstanding young men were named by Howes in connection with the young men's Who's Who, "America's Young Men," which he brought out annually. Howes discontinued the publication in 1939, and turned the idea over to the Junior Chamber.

Even a casual reading of the list of winners over the years indicates some of the great changes in American life in the past generation. In 1938, for example, one of the outstanding young men was a thirty-one-year-old pilot named Douglas Corrigan, who flew a single-engine plane across the Atlantic Ocean. Sixteen years later similar honors went to Lieutenant Colonel Charles E. Yaeger, who, at the same age, pierced the sonic barrier in an airplane and flew at the incredible speed of 1,650 miles per hour.

In the field of government, nowhere has the old adage, "coming events cast their shadows before," been more dramatically proven than in the case of these award winners: Richard M. Nixon, recognized in 1947, at the age of thirty-four, while still a Congressman; John F. Kennedy, recognized at the age of twenty-nine, also for service in Congress; Nelson Rockefeller, one of the few men who has been recognized twice, the first time at the age of thirty-three in 1941; and Harold Stassen, governor of Minnesota at the age of thirty-two, in 1939.

Here are just a few of the men named over the years. Military heroes included that one-man army, Infantry Sergeant and Congressional Medal of Honor winner Hiroshi Miyamura, twenty-four; and Navy Lieutenant Shepherd M. Jenks, who navigated the atom-powered submarine *Nautilus* under the Arctic ice cap from the Atlantic to the Pacific Ocean.

Businessmen and industrial leaders have included Edwin H. Land, thirty-one, in 1940, inventor and president of the Polaroid Corporation; Henry Ford II, twenty-nine, in 1945, president of the Ford Motor Company; and Robert A. Bowyer, twenty-one, in 1940, head of the Ford Research Laboratory, set up specifically for him.

In the academic world, Professor Arthur Schlesinger, Jr., of Harvard University, was named in 1946 at the age of twenty-nine, even before he wrote the monumental work, *The Age of Roosevelt*.

The field of sports is a natural. Bud Wilkinson, the high-principled Oklahoma football coach was named in 1949 at the age of thirty-four; Paul Brown, professional football's most successful coach, was singled out in 1942. Hamilton F. Richardson, youngest of all recipients, was twenty in 1954, and had already served as captain of the Davis Cup Team.

In the cultural field, Leonard Bernstein, later conductor of the New York Philharmonic, was named in

1944, at the age of twenty-five, and Thomas Schippers, youngest conductor ever to lead the Metropolitan Opera orchestra, in 1955, at the age of twenty-five.

In the field of entertainment, the award winner of 1938 was Rudy Vallee, then thirty-five; and just twenty-one years later, it was Pat Boone, twenty-four.

Many journalists have been recognized. Harold V. Boyle was a thirty-two-year-old working reporter when he was recognized in 1944; James Linen, one year older and one year later, was the publisher of *Time;* Warren H. Phillips, the 1959 journalist honored, managing editor of *The Wall Street Journal.* Another great name in journalism is that of C. L. Sulzberger, in 1944, at thirty-two, foreign correspondent for *The New York Times.* John H. Johnson, thirty-three in 1951, publisher of *Ebony* magazine and other publications recording the progress of Negroes, was recognized that year, and Carl T. Rowan, twenty-eight, a fearless Negro reporter two years later.

In the field of labor, James Carey, secretary of the Congress of Industrial Organizations, received the award in 1941 at the age of thirty, and Joseph A. Beirne, president of the Communications Workers of America, was honored in 1946 at the age of thirty-five.

Science and medicine have produced more winners than any other field. Dr. Thomas A. Dooley, twenty-nine in 1956, was honored for his great work in Indo-China; Dr. Albert Schatz, twenty-three in 1953, for his discovery of streptomycin; and Glenn T. Seaborg, thirty-five in 1947, for his great discoveries in nuclear chemistry.

Two presidents of the American Legion have also

been honored. They were Donald Randolph Wilson, thirty-four in 1951, and Earle Cocke, Jr., twenty-nine in 1950.

Each young man selected is presented with one of the great trophies of our time, the famous *Hands*. Their sculptor, Arthur Mayfield Craft, himself an outstanding young man in 1954, gives the message of these silver hands as: *The hope of mankind lies in the hands of youth and action.*

The most moving interpretation of the meaning of the Hands was given spontaneously by Rev. Bob Richards, himself a former recipient, in presenting the award to Charles Luckman, president of Lever Brothers. Said Bob:

"Actually, I see a great deal of the Jaycee Creed written all over these hands. . . . *We believe that faith in God gives meaning and purpose to human life.* I see the divine hand of God reaching down to touch the human hand, and in that touch there is the touch of meaning and the touch of purpose.

"These hands are filtered the other way to symbolize another great aspect of our Creed. *That the brotherhood of man transcends the sovereignty of nations.* And when you see it this way, the hand of a brother, regardless of race or creed, reaching out to embrace another, you see, I think, one of the greatest ideals in the world today.

"*We believe that economic justice is best won by free men in a free enterprise.* Actually, these hands are the unfettered hands, hands that are unshackled, hands reaching out in creativity and imagination to embrace each other in friendly competition but also to lend whatever genius that they can to every enterprise that means progress to the human race.

"*Government should be of law rather than of men.* That the greatest political ideal of history is liberty under law and these hands symbolize that too—the individual in freedom but ever cognizant of another individual.

"*Earth's great treasure lies in human personality.* Human hands—the greatest symbol of human personality, our work, our friendships, our loves.

"And, *The greatest work of man is service to humanity.* It is quite obvious those hands symbolize service."

When Richards finished and presented Luckman with the hands, so great was the emotion of the moment that Luckman could only stand in moist-eyed silence. Then he said, "I guess that I will have to say honestly that I am seldom floored. Bob, for what you are doing with your life, may I say with the utmost simplicity, I am glad your hands touched these."

The TOYM awards are made in a great ceremony, before lights, microphones, and TV cameras, climaxing a three-day celebration. Of such national importance is the event that Pat Boone, in the very peak of the entertainment season, canceled everything to fly to Fort Lauderdale, Florida, to receive the Hands in 1959. As he told the press, with obvious sincerity, pointing out that he was the first entertainer in fourteen years to receive the award, "this is the most moving thing that has ever happened to me."

But although the Ten Outstanding Young Men and their ceremony blazes in the headlines, flashes on the television screens, this is but the final moment which crowns a huge national program of recognition of young men all over the nation. For in each of the 3,700 Jaycee communities, banquets are held to honor local and state recipients of the Jaycees Distinguished Service Award. All of these 3,700 honorees each year will hardly go on to become world famous. But they will always remember that in one year of their lives they were the most outstanding young men of their communities, chosen by the men whose opinion counts most, their contemporaries.

Not as well known to the general public as the Ten Outstanding Young Men program, yet of even greater interest to the millions of Americans engaged in the world's most important business, is the more recent Outstanding Young Farmer project.

This exciting new program was born in Minnesota in 1953, the brainchild of Richard R. Quinlivan, a St. Cloud Jaycee. It was first a Minnesota program but was so successful that Jaycees nationally were quick to take it over.

The Outstanding Young Farmer project is sponsored by the American Petroleum Institute, and therein lies a story which has never previously been told. One day Ladd Haystead, the agricultural consultant to the American Petroleum Institute, and the executive secretary of the agricultural committee were running through several proposals presented to the group. The secretary read a couple of lines of the Outstanding Young Farmer proposal aloud, grunted, "We wouldn't be interested in this," crumpled the proposal up and threw it in the wastepaper basket.

Haystead promptly leaned over, fished the proposal

out of the basket, and smoothed out the crumpled pages. "Oh, but we would," he said quietly. "These young farmers are just exactly the people we want to reach!"

The search for candidates for the Outstanding Young Farmer awards begins in the summer. Says the national bulletin: "Wherever a furrow is turned, wherever a seed is growing, wherever an animal grazes, nearby there is a young man who has made outstanding progress in his agricultural career, who is rigidly practicing conservation of natural and soil resources, and who has contributed unselfishly to the well being of his fellow men."

Each year some 14,000 young farmers are nominated. The fifty state winners, with their wives, are brought together for the final awards. They do not know who will be the winner until the banquet climaxing the three day event when, one by one, the names of the winners are called.

Under these conditions, the tension builds up almost to the breaking point. One of the great dramatic moments occurred at the 1955 ceremony, held in Pittsburgh. John R. Beckstrand of North Dakota heard his name called, rose with a start, went forward and accepted his trophy. Then William A. Powell of Missouri, and A. D. Sprague, Jr., of Kentucky. Everyone looked around furtively. Whose would be the next name called?

The name was called. A pause, then a slender young man rose laboriously and started limping to the front. The hundreds of people there assembled were so quiet those in the front could hear a squeaking noise as the young man made his way. It came from the braces on his legs.

As Robert Y. Sakata, of Brighton, Colorado, went forward to receive his accolade, he could not help thinking about his past life. What irony to be here!

Bob was born in Watsonville, California, where his father had a prosperous truck farm. Then into his happy childhood came tragedy, the day of infamy, December 7, 1941. The Sakatas were torn from their land, taken to a relocation center. Finally they were settled near Brighton, Colorado, as farm laborers.

But they brought with them knowledge of farming and the willingness to work. Soon the three Sakatas, Bob, his father, and his brother, were able to lease a 40-acre farm. They raised lettuce and onions. Their crops were the best and prices were high. And then they were in an automobile accident. The father was killed.

Sometime after that, Bob was welding a piece of equipment when the acetylene torch exploded. He was burned over 80 per cent of his body. He was taken to a hospital, given up for dead. Just as a sheet was being pulled over his face, he groaned. He was still alive.

And he refused to die. But if he did live, the doctors told him at last, he would never walk again. Young Sakata listened to them without saying a word. But at night, alone in his room, no one there to stop him, he eased his tortured legs over the side of the bed and gradually put his weight on them. It was slow going, tortuous going, but after trying and falling, trying and falling, night after night after night, Bob walked.

With legs supported by braces, he went right back to

the farm, back to work. His brother died of cancer, and his brother's family became his responsibility. He carried on, a successful farmer. He met a beautiful Nisei girl, and they were married. He was active in the Presbyterian church, active in community affairs. He joined the Brighton Junior Chamber.

All this must have been going through Robert Sakata's head as he limped up to accept the trophy. As he reached the speaker's platform, words welled up into Bob Sakata's mouth. Despite a history of persecution, hardship, and incredible misfortune, they were words of heartfelt gratitude. He poured forth his appreciation to his God, for letting him live, to his country, America, and to his fellow Jaycees who had made the award possible. No record was being kept that night, and one of the greatest spontaneous speeches they ever heard anywhere will never be heard again.

But when he finished all the people there, fellow farmers, fellow Jaycees, rose to their feet in ovation. And as Bob Sakata limped back to his seat, nobody heard his braces squeak.

Young Men in Government

The luncheon of the Washington, D.C., Junior Chamber has probably attracted more big names in government and national affairs than any other weekly gathering in the nation's capital. Many a new governmental proposal or policy has been unveiled at this luncheon—and many a new young Jaycee president, presiding, has stammered and stuttered in awe of his guests.

Shortly after World War II, Arthur F. Flemming,

then chairman of the Civil Service Commission, later Secretary of Health, Education and Welfare, was a speaker at this luncheon. It was difficult for the government to attract and hold good men, he said, particularly the younger ones. He suggested a yearly award for outstanding young men in the federal government. The Jaycees took him up on the program, and it has gone over big.

As President Eisenhower said to Washington Jaycee president Kenneth W. Parkinson before the 1959 presentations: "These young men are fine examples of the challenging and rewarding careers found in the federal service. It is good to call public attention to the vital contributions being made by these and other federal employees."

Senator Hubert Humphrey of Minnesota spelled out the value of the Flemming award still further in the featured address that day. Thanking the Junior Chamber of Commerce for undertaking "this particularly fine expression of confidence and appreciation of young men in government," he went on to say: "It reflects the kind of thinking in the business community which is slowly erasing this stereotype of the 'bureaucrat in the public trough,' and replacing it with a true public understanding of the government administrator, technician, or scientist as a hardworking, enterprising, and creative individual whose contributions to his society far outweigh society's rewards."

In 1959 the Ten Outstanding Young Men in the Federal Government were chosen from over sixty final nominees in every federal agency, serving in three foreign countries, twenty-four states and the District of

Columbia. Five were from the administrative field, five from the scientific.

In 1958, one young man was flown in from Bengasi, Libya, to accept the award. He had less trouble getting to the banquet than did a man from Damascus, Maryland, only a few miles away. For a blizzard had hit the day before and transportation was stalled completely. The man from Damascus got up long before dawn and plowed through drifts for miles in order to receive his recognition as a dependable public servant.

12 | THE JCI STORY

OSCAR J. ARELLANO is a giant of a man, tall and broad, with heart to match and a driving energy. His name will live forever in the history of Asia and the free world. For Oscar was the man who appeared when destiny beckoned, the man who knew what to do and did it.

In the summer of 1954, this big Filipino architect was in Saigon, Vietnam, on his official visitation as Junior Chamber International vice-president for Asia. In a way Oscar was looking for trouble. As a Filipino, he had undergone the growing pains of a new nation cut off from its apron strings, seeking and finding democracy. As a Jaycee, he had also begun at the beginning, learning this new concept of service to mankind, working on projects to better his own war-ravaged land and its peoples.

Now Oscar had learned the joy of service, had won high office and was on his first visit through Asia. What he saw in Vietnam hit him like a blow in the solar plexus. Here was such horror and squalor, such misery, such filth, disease, and death that even this survivor of war in the Philippines was stunned and horrified.

The situation had been years in the making. For centuries the Vietnamese had known only a life of starvation and serfdom. Then had come the fight for independence and a bitter civil war between the Republic and the Communist rebels.

Finally, to cap it all, the country had been split through the middle and the northern half given to the Communists. Out of that section poured the refugees, first thousands, then hundreds of thousands. Many, victims of Communist atrocities, were sick or injured to begin with. The rest, after dragging weary feet through steaming jungle tracks, through war-torn regions which could not produce even enough food for the normal inhabitants, were little better off.

The new government of Vietnam was confused and helpless. There were only 200 doctors in the entire country, 200 doctors to care for 11 million people with every festering disease known to science. The only Vietnamese organization doing anything was the Saigon Junior Chamber, whose doctor-members were serving one hour a day in the Jaycee clinic.

Oscar Arellano left Saigon burning with a desire to help. "Here is our great chance!" he told Jaycee chapters all over Asia. "We say, in our Jaycee creed, that we believe the brotherhood of man transcends the sovereignty of nations. Let's prove it!"

It was in his homeland that his words found the most eager listeners. Here, the Filipino Jaycees saw immediately, was indeed their chance to serve. The zeal of Oscar Arellano swept the new nation. People put up money, collected medical supplies. Two prominent doctors volunteered to go to the fetid jungles of Vietnam to serve without recompense. Nurses followed their example.

The first Jaycee-sponsored medical team arrived in October. The little convoy ground through the rutted jungle roads to the village of Camau. There, in a filthy old brick building, the team set up shop and waited for patients.

None were forthcoming. People were distrustful, even hostile. Not even the expansive gestures of big-hearted Oscar Arellano could penetrate the barrier of language, fear, and even hate. But then one of the nurses got an idea. She handed a ragged urchin with washboard ribs a piece of candy, and she smiled. The child tasted and, shyly, smiled back. Another child came forward, and another. And through the smiles of the children, Operation Brotherhood began to win over the people of Vietnam.

From then on, of course, the doctors had their hands full. For these people had every disease poverty and filth can produce—tuberculosis, dysentery, cholera, malaria, festering sores and fungus, and more, many more.

Other Asian Junior Chambers were beginning to help out. Even the Jaycees of South Korea, that broken land, staged a fund-raising drive—the school children of Seoul donated their lunch money to help "our Vietnamese cousins!" Junior Chambers of Singapore, Thailand, Formosa, sent money and supplies. The Jaycees of Hong Kong, one beleaguered city huddling between the mass of Red China and the sea, contributed 5 tons of food and supplies.

The news swept Asia. Asians helping Asians! Who could believe such a thing? In India, in Malaya, on the islands of Ceylon and Formosa, from Thailand to

Tokyo, people talked about it. Word of Operation Brotherhood swept through the teeming masses of Asia like a fresh wind from the sea.

At the JCI Congress in Mexico City that year big Oscar stood up before the delegates and told them about Operation Brotherhood, about the desperate need, about the magnificent response the Filipino and Asian Jaycees had made. His enthusiasm swept the congress. Delegates from all over the world rose to their feet, and cheering, shouting, voted Operation Brotherhood the number one project of the world.

Printed material began pouring from headquarters. What was needed—exact medical supplies, multi-vitamin and vitamin B_{12} tablets for malnutrition, sulpha guanadine for intestinal disease, aureomycin for eye infections, plain old laundry soap for filth and a hundred other items. Hoes and rakes and shovels and spades, fish hooks and nets, garden seeds—corn, cabbage, carrots, tents for clinics and classrooms. And money, money, money.

How to pack, how to ship. How to adopt a village—Minneapolis Jaycees were the first foster-parents; their village was Lac-an in the province of Bien Hoa. Publicity suggestions—"Would you give a hoe if it would save the freedom of a man in Vietnam?" Sample news releases, radio and TV spot announcements; in other words, the works. And the supplies poured in.

So did people. More doctors and nurses from the Philippines, doctors, technicians, volunteers from all over the world. Administrative headquarters were set up in Saigon. One day Dave Haxton, JCI executive secretary paying an official visit, looked around the luncheon table. There were a Chinese surgeon, a Filipino social worker, Thai and Japanese nurses, a Vietnamese interpreter.

"This looks like a baby UN in session," Dave said.

There was danger not only from disease. Communist spies were everywhere, and wild beasts lived in the jungle. One day Reynaldo Maglaya, team staff officer from a remote unit, set out with a Vietnamese interpreter over the single-lane muddy road to get supplies. In the middle of the jungle, 50 miles from nowhere, night coming on, their jeep quit cold.

Maglaya built a fire, hoping to keep the jungle beasts away. As night wore on, the muffled grunts grew closer as the animals grew bolder. Suddenly, at the perimeter of the firelight, two green eyes appeared. The interpreter became hysterical. Only recently a man who had been clawed mercilessly by a tiger in the jungle had been brought in to die; Maglaya had seen what a tiger could do. He got his knife ready. At least he could try to defend himself. They stared at each other across the blaze for some time, man and beast. Finally, only God knows why, the tiger coughed, and disappeared noiselessly into the jungle.

As if things weren't bad enough, the refugee-jammed village of Quang Ngai, nestled between the forks of two rivers, was hit by a typhoon. For five weeks the town was completely isolated, and much of it was underwater. Doctors and nurses paddled native canoes along flooded streets to reach the sick. The doctor himself, weakened by over-exposure and exhaustion, was as bad off as any patient, but he relentlessly worked on. It was six weeks before the team could be relieved.

Whenever there was any kind of lull in the clinics, members of the mobile teams went out looking for patients. One afternoon Dr. Jose Alejos, head nurse Adela Pimentel, and nurses aide Yvonne Ocampo planned to visit the refugees in the village of Go-Chai, accessible only by boat up the Waico River. They were paddling up the river when the boat struck an object and capsized. Dr. Alejos tried to save the nurses, but all three drowned.

When a medical team would first come into a new community and set up their clinic in some dilapidated structure, doctors, nurses, everyone would pitch in and work. They'd scrub walls and floors on hands and knees, working even in the humid heat of midday. The Vietnamese would look at them in wonder and awe, for no Vietnamese professional man would lose face by working like a coolie.

Someday, Oscar Arellano realized, Operation Brotherhood must leave Vietnam. He began preaching a new doctrine. "We must show the Vietnamese how to take over after we are gone," he said.

And so they began trying to teach the Vietnamese how to provide for themselves. How to dig deep privies, so they would not spread their own disease. How to till the soil and plant food for their own sustenance. How to build dams, make ponds in which the prolific, nutritious native fish would thrive.

But the Vietnamese made no move to carry out these suggestions. They had been oppressed too long to care. And so the doctors and nurses grabbed pick and shovel, dug those privies themselves. They made crude incinerators of mud and burned all garbage. They hoed and raked plots of ground, planted seed, carried water.

Gradually, it sunk in. Timidly, one by one, the Vietnamese would take a pick or shovel, grab a rake. And when the gardens produced rich, energy-producing foods, the battle was won.

"The way to teach these people," said a Filipino doctor with a lucrative practice back home, proudly showing his calloused hands, "is down on your knees, digging."

Operation Brotherhood began among apathetic, almost lifeless people. Two years later it ended with those same people dreaming, planning, working with a new energy, a new enthusiasm, a new hope. Operation Brotherhood had brought a new land into the brotherhood of nations.

Although the idea of Operation Brotherhood was born in the mind of one man, not even Oscar Arellano could have carried it out alone. He had the entire Junior Chamber International, then 57 nations strong, behind him.

At that time, JCI was barely ten years old. The Junior Chamber movement, however, had begun spreading in the twenties. In 1926, a representative of Canada's big Winnepeg local attended the United States national convention in Jacksonville, Florida, and ever since then Winnepeg has proudly boasted: "We're the chapter that made the Junior Chamber International!"

Three years later, the president of England's Northhampton Junior Chamber of Commerce visited the United States. Correspondence was set up between American Junior Chambers and eleven English Junior

Chambers. Locals were started in New Zealand, Australia, Mexico, and Colombia.

World War II brought a great desire for hemisphere solidarity to the new world. William M. Shepherd from Little Rock, Arkansas, U.S. Jaycee president in 1942–43 and Allyn Taylor, Canadian national Jaycee president, felt that the time had come to extend the Junior Chamber throughout the Americas. They set about arranging an organizational tour through Central America. In the eight months it took to get everything worked out Taylor studied Spanish and became a proficient conversationalist. Shepherd chose a Colorado Springs Jaycee named Vance Graham, who spoke Spanish fluently, to go along as adviser and interpreter.

Arranging such a trip in wartime had its problems. At first things went smoothly. Shepherd obtained the enthusiastic support of Nelson Rockefeller, coordinator of Inter-American affairs. Passports and official letters of introduction were obtained. Many Jaycee publications and programs were translated into Spanish for the trip. High priorities for air travel were obtained.

Finally it came time for the trip. Then, suddenly, all their priorities were canceled. Shepherd had no way of knowing, then, that every piece of equipment was being tied up in order to get some 3,000 special agents to Casablanca for the meeting between President Roosevelt and Prime Minister Churchill. All he knew was that the Jaycee delegation was expected in Mexico City, and he had to get it there. It took some high-level finagling, involving a quick conference with a top transportation official at a party in Washington after midnight, but he got those priorities.

Then came trouble at the border. The three Jaycees would be permitted to go across, but they couldn't take their briefcases full of important letters and introductions and carefully translated program material. It took hours of arguing, from soft-voiced cajolery to shouted threats, frantic long distance telephone calls to officials in three nations, and out-and-out bribery to get the officials to relent. But they still would not permit Shepherd to take his briefcase containing the letters of introduction. Finally Shepherd agreed to leave his briefcase with the customs officials. He quickly and furtively took out the most important letters and secreted them about his person. And finally the three North American Jaycees were in Mexico.

They found the young men throughout Central America most receptive to Jaycee plans. Arrangements were made for an Inter-American Congress in Mexico City and there, on December 11, 1944, Junior Chamber International was officially born. As some Latin American countries have strict regulations on organizations dealing with activities pertaining to commerce, the word "commerce" was omitted from the international title.

After the organization meeting, the first real JCI Congress was held in Panama City in February, 1946, after World War II had come to a close. There probably has been no congress like it since, for the delegates of the host city picked up the tab for everything, and in Panama City, at least for a JCI World Congress, everything means *everything*.

The JCI grew slowly over the years. Only twelve nations sent delegates to Brussels in 1949, but one of those nations was the United States with 132 delegates. Following the JCI meeting they toured Europe as part of "Operation Democracy" spreading the truth about life in the United States under free government, and stimulating interests in the Junior Chamber movement.

At the 1951 World Congress in Montreal, Philip P. R. Pugsley of Canada was elected president, and Horace Henderson of the United States was named vice-president for North America. Robert Ladd, the U.S. Jaycees' brilliant executive vice-president, became acting secretary general. Under this triumverate, the JCI picked up speed. Horace Henderson, with the true missionary spirit, made his famous year-long trip around the world, organizing Junior Chambers wherever he went. In 1954, with Douglas L. Hoge of the United States as president and Philip N. Van Slyck, Jr., as full-time secretary general, the world organization enjoyed its greatest year. At the JCI Congress that year, Horace Henderson was named the Outstanding Jaycee of the World, and Oscar Arellano proposed Operation Brotherhood.

Weapon of the Free World

Today JCI operates on a budget of $142,000. A third of this goes to publishing the JCI *World,* with a circulation of over 75,000, printed in English, Spanish, French and Japanese.

A fourth of the budget expenses goes for travel of the JCI president and vice-presidents. These vice-presidents represent Asia, Europe, North America, northern Latin America, South America, Oceania, and Africa. They all cover their territory, and their president covers the world. The airline ticket Maurice Sexton bought for one of his world tours was twenty-eight feet long!

The world secretariat is located in Miama Beach, Florida. Several cities bid for the permanent headquarters, with Hong Kong and New York making extremely attractive offers, but Miami Beach won out.

United States Jaycees have by far the greatest membership in JCI, and their dues make up 90 per cent of JCI's total income. But they don't run the organization, far from it. The United States, with some 3,700 chapters, has just exactly seven votes. Hong Kong, with just exactly one chapter, has two votes. JCI was put together at the very beginning so that neither of the two largest blocs, the English-speaking nations and Spanish-and-Portuguese-speaking nations, can control it. And this is just exactly the way Canada and the United States would have it.

Although the United States has furnished more international presidents than any other country, three, the Philippines, New Zealand and Mexico are all pushing close, with two. First JCI president was Raul Garcia Vidal of Mexico, 1944; Erasmo Chambonnet of Panama, 1946; Taylor Cole of the U.S.A. (Dallas, Texas), 1947; Victor Boucas of Brazil, 1948; Theo Staar of Belgium, 1949; Ramon V. Des Rosario of the Philippines, 1950; Philip P. R. Pugsley of Canada, 1951; Roberto Villanueva of the Philippines, 1952; Douglas L. Hoge of the U.S.A. (Cincinnati, Ohio),

1953; Peter B. Watts of New Zealand, 1954; A. de Oliveira Sales of Hong Kong, 1955; Ira D. Kaye of the U.S.A. (Los Angeles), 1956; Alberto Philippe of Mexico, 1957; Maurice Sexton of New Zealand, 1958.

By no means is Junior Chamber activity the same all over the world. The Junior Chambers of England and Scotland are, literally, junior chambers of commerce, and pay strict attention to business affairs. England, as a matter of fact, pulled out of JCI for a couple of years. Most of the other countries of the world follow the broader North American pattern.

One great American influence has been in the committee system of operation. Other countries just don't seem to use committees. Secretary General Robert P. Green was once talking about the work of various committees with a JCI vice-president from another country, when the vice-president interrupted him.

"Why," he asked, "do you keep saying *committees?* Don't you mean chapters?"

For the first time, Green, who had been active in JCI for several years, realized that even the top echelon leadership of the JCI did not understand its workings. At that moment, too, he understood something that had been puzzling him all along. Frequently JCI headquarters would receive different letters from different committees of the same Junior Chamber, yet all these would be signed by the same man, the president. Now he caught on. They just didn't understand committees.

Green started explaining the committee set up, and suddenly he saw the light flash on in the other man's eyes. "Oh, you mean that each committee is like a little chapter within the chapter!"

And so a JCI vice-president learned for the first time how to appoint a committee.

The growing American interest in non-partisan political activities has also spread. As a matter of fact, Jaycee activity in the Philippines was only technically non-partisan. For when the Philippine Jaycees went out and beat the drums in a powerful and impressive campaign for clean government, there was no question whatsoever in the minds of the people what candidate they were for—because Ramon Magsaysay was the candidate who stood for clean government. And Magsaysay swept into office with an overwhelming majority, for which he publicly credited the Jaycees.

Another idea perhaps not exclusively American but certainly popular in America, is just good old companionship. When some of the members of the Saigon Junior Chamber passed the age limit of the Jaycees and missed the camaraderie of a civic organization, they did something about it—organized a Rotary Club!

But the great significance of the Junior Chamber International is that it has proven and will continue to prove that young men can indeed change the world. JCI has broken down the barriers of centuries. It was the French Junior Chamber which proposed the West German Junior Chamber for membership in JCI, seconded by Belgium.

JCI has broken down the barriers of hate and vengeance. At a regional conference in Hong Kong a group of Jaycees from Thailand, Burma, the Philippines, and Malaya were getting down to business when six young men, delegates from the latest Asian country to join JCI, shyly entered the conference room. They were Japanese, and almost every delegate present came from a country which had been ravaged by Japanese forces.

Sometime later the question of where the next conference would be held came to a vote. The choice was unanimous—Tokyo!

"We felt," a Filipino Jaycee who had once sworn to kill every Japanese he met explained later, "that holding the conference in Japan would give the new Japanese Junior Chamber a big boost in morale. And besides, those Japanese Jaycees turned out to be pretty good guys, and we knew the decision would please them."

Many of the new Jaycee nations are jumping, in one generation, from eighteenth-century colonialism to the twentieth century. JCI is helping them make that transition. JCI helps them develop leaders who think in twentieth-century terms.

These national leaders are coming along even faster than JCI predictions. Roberto Villanueva once said:

"We are unshakable in the conviction that from among the ranks of the Jaycees today will come the leaders of their countries tomorrow."

It was not long after that Jaycee Somphong Tipisansarakit took over the armed forces of Thailand!

Many JCI leaders, mature men who reached the top levels in the Junior Chambers of their own countries before going into the international, and who have studied it carefully, have made thoughtful, interesting comments on Junior Chamber International.

This is what they have said:

Phil Pugsley: "Junior Chamber International can become the most important non-military weapon of the free world."

Arnaldo de Oliveiro Sales: "We Jaycees are on the threshold of a new word to conquer. We Jaycees are already engaged in the battle for the minds of the young people, conscious that lasting peace can only be achieved when the desire for it is genuine in the minds and hearts of men."

Doug Hoge: "JCI has become, whether we like it or not, a mature and vital force respected by free men everywhere in the world."

Doug Hoge again, summing up the whole idea of Junior Chamber International, used these inspiring words: "Politics are irrelevant if men are hungry, naked, sick, illiterate and without hope. Four-fifths of the population of the world is underprivileged in just these basic ways. They do not care *who* promised them 'pie in the sky,' but they insist on a basic subsistence diet. They want clothing and shelter. They want the tools of education. And they want to feel hope for the future.

"Junior Chamber is a non-political idea which offers them that hope. It offers self-help. It offers a way in which the underprivileged can solve their own basic problems—through democratic methods, through the principles of joint action and community-wide cooperation. Junior Chamber demands no special political loyalty, exacts no particular religious, racial or nationalistic allegiance. It is simply good citizenship in action, anywhere. It is the idea which says, 'take what tools you have, join with your neighbors and do the job your community needs done.' It is the idea which can drive want, fear and hopelessness from the hearts of those who will grasp and use it."

Junior Chamber International

Country	Chapters	Membership
Argentina	13	620
Australia	130	6,150
Belgium	11	1,200
Bermuda	1	69
Bolivia	3	120
Brazil	8	562
Burma	1	60
Canada	269	18,000
Ceylon	9	350
China	4	300
Colombia	7	127
Costa Rica	5	180
Cuba	3	150
Ecuador	6	300
El Salvador	1	47
England and N. Ireland	47	4,000
Fiji	1	31
Finland	6	160
France	32	1,200
Germany	95	6,000
Guatemala	6	300
Honduras	11	300
Hong Kong	1	158
India	21	700
Ireland	2	230
Israel	10	400
Italy	3	150
Japan	160	7,110
Korea	3	225
Laos	6	112
Malaya	5	203

Country	Chapters	Membership
Mexico	56	1,476
Morocco	2	75
Netherlands	3	90
New Zealand	80	5,100
Nicaragua	3	84
Norway	1	20
Pakistan	2	37
Panama	4	100
Paraguay	1	41
Peru	10	500
Philippines	43	2,000
Portugal	1	35
Puerto Rico	3	170
Saar	1	57
Sarawak	2	88
Scotland	7	1,082
Singapore	1	80
Sweden	3	182
Thailand	3	400
Union of South Africa	11	700
United States of America	3,778	200,000
Uruguay	1	70
Venezuela	1	35
Vietnam	11	450

There are also Junior Chambers in the following countries, though not affiliated with JCI: Afghanistan, Barbados, Cambodia, Central African Federation, Chile, Cyprus, Denmark, Dominican Republic, Ethiopia, Ghana, Greece, Guam, Haiti, Iceland, Indonesia, Iraq, Iran, Jamaica, Jordan, Kenya, Lebanon, Liberia, Madagascar, Mauritius, Nigeria, North Borneo, Okinawa, Spain, Switzerland, Turkey, United Arab Republic, and the Virgin Islands.

_13_ | _THEY'RE NOT CRAZY—_
THEY'RE JAYCEES!

WE BELIEVE ... _that service to humanity is the best work of life._

Bill Brownfield never dreamed, when he wrote those immortal words, that they would provide both the impetus and the reason for young men in foreign lands to change the very philosophy and purpose of their lives. Those few words have shattered ways of thought built up over centuries.

In many areas of the world, people just don't do things for other people without recompense. The thrill and inner satisfaction of serving humanity is unknown. Mankind operates on the cynical premise that people help people only when they want something. It follows, therefore, that if anyone does do something for anyone else, without hope of personal gain, he must be pretty much of a fool.

What can men of goodwill do in the face of such tradition? Unfortunately, for too many years, they have been unable to do anything. And then, into many of these regions of the world burst, like a new sun, this vibrant idea, the Jaycee creed. As more and more solid and respectable young men joined this organization, as they went on to become community and national leaders, their strange new idea of service to mankind became more and more acceptable. You could help your neighbor, even when, as in Operation Brotherhood, your neighbor was half a world away, without being considered a fool!

Time and time again, as more Junior Chambers are organized throughout the world, it becomes obvious that within the human breast lies a fervent desire to be of service to humanity, to join in the best work of life. When a Junior Chamber is formed, its young men are then able to go out and do good in its name without being suspected or ridiculed. And they leap at the opportunity.

In Guadalajara, Mexico, a group of young men were talking one day. One of them, in a rare outburst of confidence, revealed that he was concerned about some of the children in the community—children so poor that they trudged off to school each morning with no breakfast at all in their bellies.

Another young man shot him a quick suspicious glance, saw that he really was serious, and then softly said, "I, too, have thought the same thing, many times."

In a matter of minutes they all agreed that it would be a wonderful thing to send those *muchachos* off to school with a full stomach, even if it would be the only time during the day that such a marvelous condition would exist. But then they shook their heads sadly. Even if they had everything it would take—money, organization, kitchens, supplies—to carry on the project it would still be impossible. The whole town would oppose the project, if only because they didn't understand it. And the parents of the children themselves, no matter how poor they might be, would never permit their children to be exposed to such obvious trickery.

But wait—perhaps there was an answer. Had not the young men heard of this strange new movement, the Asociación de Cámaras Junior de México?

And so the young men of Guadalajara organized their own Cámara Junior. They raised money and set up kitchens. And from then on every poor kid of Guadalajara has gone to school with a full stomach. The 3-millionth breakfast was served in 1959, and the program was still growing. And nobody thought the young men were crazy, either—they were just Jaycees!

Similar projects are carried on all over the JCI world, on local, state, national, and international levels. The JCI secretariat has distributed some 400 separate programming units over the years, of which Operation Brotherhood was, of course, by far the most successful. Some 70,000 items, published in English, Spanish, and French, advising Jaycees all over the world on how they can serve mankind are sent out from national headquarters each year.

But it is the local individual projects which are the most fascinating of all—sometimes because they are so similar, sometimes because they are so different.

In Panama City the Junior Chamber's tree-planting project could have been picked up and moved, as is, from any other community, even down to a carefully posed picture of four top-level Jaycees and His Honor the Mayor, all staring hard at one forlorn little twig. A Havana project was a more unique one, both in its original purpose and eventual application. In an effort to cut down on automobile collisions at Havana's extremely blind corners the Jaycees put up mirrors at each corner, on an angle, so you could see what was coming down the side streets. Then came the Revolution and both government forces and rebels used the mirrors to direct snipers in taking pot shots at the opposition.

Jaycees in Johannesburg carry on another unique project. It might come in handy in case you're thinking of going into the African bush to trade with the natives. It is a school for traders.

In Wellington, New Zealand, Jaycees collect old razor blades for a local trader who uses them for barter with South Sea Island natives. Lepers on the island of Borneo can thank the Sarawak Jaycees for the Saturday night movies.

Let's skip around the world, looking at Jaycee projects both usual and unusual, beginning with commerce and industry. You will be pleased to know that in England, the Portsmouth Junior Chamber has staged its first management-training course. A report on the Central Electricity Authority and Gas Council can be obtained from the Hon. Secretary of the Exeter Junior Chamber. The legal and finance section of the Liverpool Junior Chamber put on an interesting discussion of investment clubs.

Contests were hot and heavy in the National Debating Competition. In one contest, Portsmouth met Bristol at the Salisbury Guild Hall and proposed: "That it would have been better if the Plymouth Rock had landed upon the Pilgrim fathers instead of the Pilgrim fathers on Plymouth Rock."

The Bristol team won the debate, fortunately for international relations.

A most interesting work, *How to Save Dollars in Hong Kong!,* has been compiled by a special committee of the Hong Kong Junior Chamber of Commerce. It tells you such things as the advantages of buying a cooperative flat in the city as opposed to building a home in the New Territories, whether to put your savings into gold or U.S. dollars.

The Grimsby, England, Jaycees also published a book, this one on the business and commercial life of their community with an eye toward attracting new business. And if you're thinking of building a new plant in France, La Jeune Chambre de St. Omer has published a survey of their town, telling you just about anything you'd need to know.

Jaycees in Dundee, Scotland, apparently want you to have a good time. Their survey lists only hotel accommodations and entertainment facilities. And the survey of the Cámara Junior of Tela, Honduras, gives a comprehensive description of the facilities of the port.

The Manila, Philippines, Jaycees prepare weekly articles for publication in the *Manila Times* and *Fookien Times* of which JCI ex-president Roberto Villanueva is publisher. All the Junior Chambers on the island of Mindanao in the Philippines combined into one group in order to make a survey on farming, industry, and rural development.

Trade fairs are constantly being held over the world. The JCI Economic Affairs Commission keeps tabs on them for you. Whether in Brussels or Hyderabad, Kuala Lumpur or any West German town, you'll find an EAC representative ready to show you around.

Just as the Outstanding Young Farmer program began in Minnesota and was taken over by national, so was the Adelaide Jaycees' Apprentice-of-the-Year program taken over by Australia. The lucky winner spends a full year in England as a reward. The British Junior Chamber sends their number one apprentice to Australia in exchange.

Finland Jaycees conduct an excellent management program. So do the Jaycees of Israel, as well as a large course in public speaking. If you would like to read about "Brainstorming" in Hebrew, the Israel Jaycees have just what you're looking for. They translated it from the standard JCI manual.

Jaycees in many French communities have staged seminars advocating the European Common Market, which would break down economic barriers between France, Belgium, Luxembourg, West Germany, and Italy.

The world's Jaycees are also active in the field of health. The Nadiad Junior Chamber of India, founded with eight members, immediately began Operation Surgical Camp. In its first year it performed 206 tonsillectomies in five surrounding towns.

When 1958 JCI president Alberto Philippe visited India, his eyes were opened wide by all the fine work the Junior Chamber was doing all across the country. One of the institutions he visited was the Junior Chamber dispensary at Chintadripet, supported by the Madras chapter, where doctors see an average of 100 people every day during the year.

Into the small colony of Hong Kong, every day,

pour at least 300 refugees from Communist China.
How can medical care possibly be provided for so
many people?

Jaycees have furnished part of the answer. They saw
that on the tiny island of Peng Chau there were 4,000
inhabitants but no water main, no drainage system, no
medical facilities. Starting from scratch, with plans
drawn up by Jaycee architect Ping K. Ng, the Jaycees
put up and outfitted a handsome building—largest
building on the island—which amply serves the needs
of Peng Chau's people.

In just a few months, the 37 members of the Strasbourg, France, Junior Chamber, which had been organized less than a year, processed over 12,000 Hungarian refugees who poured into the small town after
the Hungarian revolt was so brutally put down by
Russia. The Red Cross turned operations over entirely
to the Jaycees. The convoys, containing hundreds of
despondent, ill, and homeless people, including many
children, nearly always arrived in the middle of the
night. The Strasbourg Jaycees were both efficient and
sympathetic, apportioning food, clothing, shelter, and
medical care to the homeless victims.

Jaycees frequently do such a good job that they have
to continue, even take on more duties. Jaycees in El
Salvador, which had no mental institution at all prior
to 1953, recognized the need and built a fine mental
hospital. Then they could find no one capable of taking
over the administration. There was only one answer
to the problem. Since 1953 the entire board of directors
has been composed entirely of Jaycees.

In Australia Jaycees saw the need for flying ambulances to serve the remote country "out back." A national project resulted in $14,000, and a plane was bought and outfitted. And what else could its call letters be but AJC?

In Guatemala nine JCI senators got together and established a countrywide system of blood collection centers. They maintain blood banks in six Guatemala cities.

What is probably the most difficult blood bank project of all time took place in Calcutta, India, where so many divergent religious faiths come together. Despite the great differences, the Jaycees were able to please nearly everybody, and establish a successful blood bank.

The Jaycees of Durban, South Africa, also seeking to establish a blood bank, heard of Calcutta's success. They wrote for information, which was immediately forthcoming. At the time of the correspondence, anti-Indian feeling was running high in Durban and many Indians were attacked and beaten. Durban was hardly popular with the people of India as a result. Yet the Jaycees of both Durban and Calcutta ignored the situation completely when it came to a matter of service to mankind.

From the field of community health it's a short step to community betterment, and Jaycees knock themselves out for their communities the world over. How many parks, playgrounds, libraries, have been contributed to communities through Jaycee endeavor? The number is legion.

Most active Jaycee chapters have been the seven junior Chambers in wartorn Korea, where Jaycees have been not only raising funds, but actually getting out and working on demolition of ruins, construction of schools, hospitals and public buildings.

In Ozamiz City, Philippines, Jaycees built a handsome social hall and public swimming pool, relandscaped the civic center, painted city hall, put up street signs, and, in passing, set up Junior Chambers in three nearby communities, all in one year.

New Junior Chambers love to think of their own projects. When Dave Haxton got together with some Ethiopians in Addis Ababa to talk about starting a Jaycee chapter, he refused to make suggestions, instead encouraged them to do their own thinking about what the community needed. One of the young men shyly proposed the establishment of small libraries in the poorest section of the city. Haxton said the idea sounded great. The young men immediately took off on their own. They'd begun work on two libraries before the Addis Ababa Junior Chamber was in existence.

In Rio de Janeiro, 1959 JCI Congress city, hydrophobia became a serious problem. The Jaycees put on a big contest to name the King of the Street Dogs. Seems that every body in Rio showed up with a dog. The King was crowned, and, incidentally, 25,000 dogs were inoculated against rabies.

In Mindanao, Philippines, the Filipino chapter organized a huge rat-extermination program. They gave prizes for the biggest, the longest, the most rats brought in. They formed rat-killing gangs in the countryside, fumigated rats in the city. The extermination program was a success.

The Jaycees of Kawasaki, Japan, are the undisputed champions when it comes to clean-up campaigns. They turned out a bucket-and-broom brigade of 10,000 citizens, who scrubbed the whole town, from top to bottom, in one day.

In Ceylon, the five Jaycee chapters—Colombo, Mt. Lavinia, Kandy, Galle, and Matara—were busy enough, with projects ranging from rehabilitation of delinquent children to establishing a Jaycee dance band, when disaster struck. Flood swept over a large portion of the island. The Junior Chamber was the first organization on the scene. Jaycees raised $50,000, distributed 150 tons of relief goods. And then they set out on a long-range rehabilitation program.

In Singapore the Jaycees put up their community hall, modern and complete, built for all the citizens of the town. The Villa Maria, Argentina, Jaycees, haven't gotten around to putting up a convention hall yet, preferring more basic projects. They constructed a combination telephone building and post office for the community!

Wherever you find Jaycees, you find them doing things for kids. Youth welfare programs exist all around the world, but the tendency is more to better educational facilities and better libraries than to playgrounds and swimming pools.

It may make American parents feel just a little bit better to know that in Hong Kong parents have the same problem: What to do about comic books? In Hong Kong many of the kids devouring horror comics have never been to school, can read nothing else. In the face of this situation Hong Kong Jaycees have done a fantastic job with Operation Library. In the period of five years they established 12 permanent Jaycee libraries for underprivileged children, carrying each library through from the very selection of the site to completing and stocking it. Four thousand youngsters visit these libraries every day. In the villages the kids get their books from the Jaycee library van.

Youth welfare is particularly important in Morocco, Casablanca Jaycees report; half the population of Morocco are teen-agers! Jaycees have lowered the age of their leadership-training program so that teen-agers can attend.

Japanese Jaycees are particularly proud of the artistic talents of Japanese children. They have sent displays of children's art to over 100 JCI member nations and individual chapters.

Many Jaycee chapters all over the world sponsor orphanages or help the kids in one way or another. Jaycees of Chittagong, Pakistan, entertaining some 200 orphans at their annual outing, learned of an unhappy situation. Orphans leaving the home because of the age limit couldn't get jobs; they had learned no trade. The Jaycees immediately began work on an industrial home to provide practical training. One of its products is cane furniture, made to Filipino standards. For since Filipinos are famous for cane work, Chittagong Jaycees went to Manila Jaycees for complete information on the subject.

The Mexico City Jaycees sponsor a rehabilitation school for handicapped children. Its curriculum includes teaching blind children to read and write Braille.

JCI's Education and Youth Activities Commission

is naturally one of its busiest. It includes the JCI International Scholarship Exchange Program—ISEP—in which Jaycees of one country make scholarships available to students of another. China, for example, makes available two scholarships to Japanese students. Hong Kong brings in students from Malaya, Sarawak, Singapore, and Mauritius. Peru—specifically the Junior Chambers of Callao and Lima—has brought in students from Bolivia and Ecuador. And so it goes, all around the world.

And do not forget Christmas. Although Jaycees around the world are of many different faiths, Christmas seems to be everywhere. In 1959 the EYAC world chairman made the official announcement that Christmas programs had been conducted in Australia, Canada, Colombia, England, Hong Kong, New Zealand, Nicaragua Puerto Rico, Philippines, Singapore, Peru, and the United States. It might be of significance to point out that the proud chairman that year was Moshe Meron, of Israel.

14

"WE MADE THE JUNIOR CHAMBER INTERNATIONAL!"

A VISITOR to the Canadian House of Commons, watching the smooth, orderly proceedings on the floor, might not realize that the Canadian Junior Chamber of Commerce was largely responsible for the efficient operations of this august body. The secret lies in the pair of earphones you see handy on each member's desk.

For Canada, of course, is a country of two official languages, English and French. Although it presents a broad and dependable front on international issues, still regional differences were for a long time exaggerated and confused by the fact that many legislators didn't know what the others were talking about.

Back in 1951 many Canadian Jaycees saw what could be done in such a situation. That year the JCI Congress met in Montreal. With Jaycees from all over the world in attendance, it was imperative that simultaneous translation be used. Interpreters were recruited and trained, and a system of microphones and earphones installed. And so, when a Jaycee delegate stood up to make an impassioned speech in English, French, Spanish, Portuguese, German, Japanese, or what have you, other delegates could follow him almost simultaneously in their own languages.

It worked so well that the Canadian Jaycees set up

a similar system for their national convention at Regina. It was built by the Arnprior, Ontario, Jaycees, and financed by the neighboring Sonya chapter. This equipment, Canadian Jaycees now agree, was largely instrumental in cementing the solid relations which now exist between the Junior Chamber of Commerce and La Chambre de Commerce des Jeunes. The equipment has since been used at all national conventions, and even made the trip to Edinburgh for the 1955 World Congress.

And then the Shawinigan Falls, Quebec, Jaycees got a great idea. If we Jaycees can do it, they said, why can't our country do it too? They presented a resolution to that effect at the Halifax national convention. It was passed. Ross Smyth of Montreal, national Jaycee president that year, officially presented the idea to the Speaker of the House, René Beaudouin. The equipment was installed and is today helping to bring about an even greater rapport between the peoples of Canada, thanks to the Canadian Jaycees.

Though it took a few years longer for the national organization to get under way, there have been Junior Chambers in Canada almost as long as in the United States. First local unit was founded in 1923 at Winnipeg and the Jaycee movement spread out rapidly from there. Today there are some 270 chapters, with over 20,000 members. It operates on an $80,000 budget. National headquarters is at Montreal, where, incidentally, the largest chapter, the Montreal French-speaking unit, 1,200 strong, is also located.

Canadian Jaycees operate just like all other Jaycees, only, in some respects, more so. Canada's participation

in Operation Brotherhood, for example, was tremendous; the Winnipeg Jaycees raffled off a house and contributed $6,000 from this one project alone.

The Jaycees of Kamloops, British Columbia, staged
a successful blood-donor campaign with 1,024 people
contributing one pint of blood each, all in one day. Just
like any other Jaycee campaign—except that the tem-
perature that day was 30 below zero.

Canadian projects are big, all right. The Jaycees of
Fort William, Ontario, population 35,000, raised $110,-
000 for a hockey arena. Toronto Jaycees started the
spring clean-up campaign by painting a whole house
in one hour, then led a mighty march on City Hall,
with the participants carrying brooms, mops, or rakes.

And when the national organization staged an all-
Canada banquet at the Minneapolis JCI World Congress, it was unquestionably the most talked about event
of the Congress. They served everything from New-
foundland cod's tongue to a ton of rich, red Alberta
beef.

Canadian beautification is a continuing national
project. In acknowledgment of it the Canadian Paint,
Varnish, and Lacquer Association, suddenly realizing
with an icy chill where their industry would be if it
weren't for the Jaycees, presented 1959 national president Jack O'Rourke with a handsome clock for Jaycee
headquarters.

The Safe Driving Road-e-o is also a big Canadian
national project. It is sponsored by the All-Canada Insurance Federation and Imperial Oil Limited. Over
15,000 boys participate each year.

Sometimes the Jaycees undertake projects which

prove to be somewhat ambitious. The Prince George, British Columbia, Jaycees, hearing that the famous British Grenadier Guards were having trouble getting bearskins for their tall headgear, set out to rectify the situation with a twenty-five-man hunting party. Three Jaycees got lost and another shot himself in the foot, but not a bear bit the dust.

However, the Jaycees stuck to the project. They raised money, bought pelts from professional hunters, and the Grenadier Guards still march.

The Swift Current, Saskatchewan, Jaycees decided that they would build a tenting area for tourists. Older, wiser heads attempted to dissuade them. Why in the world would tourists want to stop in Swift Current? But the Jaycees went ahead. They talked the city out of five acres, raised $3,000 as a starter. The first year they leveled the land, seeded the area, planted some trees, built fences. Next they put in parking areas, each one shielded by trees and shrubs, put up a building housing restrooms, shower rooms, and an information office, and installed outdoor lighting.

Their first summer of operation they had 500 campers from all provinces and most of the states, as well as from other parts of the British Empire.

In Goderich, Ontario, the Jaycees did more than merely ignore older and wiser counsel. Informed by the senior Board of Trade that it was too late to do anything about Goderich's declining fortunes, the Juniors got their dander up and set out to prove different. They surveyed the town, determined what it had to offer, then contacted companies in both Canada and the United States. The Schaefer Pen Company became

interested, looked the town over, and built a million-
dollar plant with a payroll of 175 local people as a result. The senior Board of Trade died a natural death
but the Jaycees resurrected it.

Canada has produced many success stories. Michael
Starr, Minister of Labor, William McL. Hamilton,
Postmaster General, and Arnold D. Heeney, Ambas-
sador to the United States, were all Jaycees.

When Ross Smyth was national Jaycee president, he
sat down one day with Mayor Don McKay of Calgary,
president of the Canadian Federation of Mayors, to
work out the year's program of civic affairs courses.
"Don't be nervous," McKay told him with a grin,
"just ten years ago I had your job."

Smyth's story, incidentally, is a typical example of
how the Junior Chamber can change a young man's
life. Shy, with only a high school education, he joined
the Montreal Junior Board of Trade purely for the
speaking course. He was put on the Civic Affairs committee, then studying the financial reports of the local
transportation company. Smyth couldn't make heads
or tails of them, so he enrolled in night school to learn,
and wound up with a degree in commerce.

In the meantime he learned to speak and started up
the Jaycee ladder. At the time he had a technical job
with Trans-Canada Airlines as a flight dispatcher. After
he had made speeches all over Canada as Jaycee president, the company set up a Speakers Bureau and put
him in charge of it.

As national president, Smyth traveled well over 150,-
000 miles, keeping a diary. Here are a few excerpts.

February 23: National Vice Pres. Louis Reid drives me
from Chicoutimi to Hébertville Station . . . reception
at Town Hall 10:30 A.M. . . . 11:15 A.M. another reception at Notre Dame de Hébertville. . . . 12:30 reception and dinner at St. Jerome with St. Gedeon
Jaycees present . . . Mayor Demoules. . . . 3 P.M. reception in church basement of Desbiens-Mills . . . Louis
helps me amend French notes between stops . . . ar-
rive Alma 5:30 P.M.—civic reception . . . drive to
Jonquière by 8:30—met at suburbs by police motor-
cycle escort . . . face off puck at hockey game. . . . I
draw winning ticket on ice and a Miss Tremblay won
a '56 Buick! . . . address mixed Jaycee meeting at
11:00 P.M. . . . special traffic safety meeting and say
few words on behalf of JC at 12:30 A.M.! Police Chief
Decaire proudly shows me around his new cells!

February 24: Drive from Jonquière to Normandin (90
miles) for 11 A.M. reception. . . . 1 P.M. reception and
dinner Misstassini—JC pres and Curé next to me
speak no English! . . . then to Dolbeau at 3:30 P.M. to
meet Mayor and sign book. . . . 5:30 P.M. reception
at Roberbal . . . many cocktails . . . at 8:45 P.M. attend
big civic reception St. Felicien . . . to president's home
. . . back to Jonquière by 3 A.M.

February 25: Off for Three Rivers by 8 A.M. . . .

After visiting over 120 Junior Chambers the length
and breadth of Canada, Smyth had a pertinent observa-
tion to make on the customs of his countrymen.

"I've never been offered a drink in the office of an
English-speaking mayor," he said with a grin, "but
I've never been in a French-speaking mayor's office
when I wasn't!"

15 | WHEN HUSBAND AND WIFE WORK TOGETHER AS ONE ...

THE JUNIOR CHAMBER OF COMMERCE, in any and all countries, constantly faces a serious problem, one shared by corporations, other organizations, even governments. The problem is, in a word, wives.

To get to the top of any Jaycee level, local, state, national, or international, to derive the full benefits of leadership training the Junior Chamber has to offer, the Jaycee must be willing to put in time. There is no other way. Sometimes it means spending from one to seven evenings a week away from home for weeks on end. It means weekends, holidays, vacations.

How many men who could have reached the heights in the Junior Chamber—or business, or public office— have failed to fulfill their destiny because their wives wanted them at home nights? The number is uncountable. Nor is it possible to estimate how many top leaders in any enterprise would never have made the climb if it hadn't been for the inspiration, understanding, encouragement and, in some cases, whip-cracking of the wife back home.

Many wives of top-ranking Jaycees candidly admit that they were displeased or even hurt and angry when their husbands first climbed on board the Jaycee treadmill. It was only when they really understood the real importance of the Junior Chamber to the country, the community, and their husband's career that they began encouraging their Jaycees on to greater efforts.

In many communities Jaycee wives have become so interested in their husbands' activities that they have organized or joined the Junior Chamber's auxiliary. There are today auxiliaries in nearly every state. They are known variously as Jaycettes, Jaycee-ettes, Jaynes, Jaynettes, Jay-dettes, and Mrs. Jaycees, with "Jaycettes" the most popular. In Wisconsin, where the first auxiliary was formed in Oshkosh in 1933 and the first state auxiliary formed in 1937 (Beaver Dam, Oshkosh, Rhinelander, and Wasau were the charter members), "Jaycettes" is registered with the secretary of state.

A national organization was formed in 1947 with fifteen states as members, but it lasted only a year.

Why should a Jaycee's wife be a Jaycette? Mrs. Kenneth Cornell, 1958–59 president of the Wisconsin Jaycettes, has made a long list of reasons. First of all, Molly says, the wife understands better the importance of her husband's Jaycee activities. She can join with him on many projects, such as the Easter egg hunt, in enthusiasm and togetherness. She gains an insight into his business world. She makes new friends, enjoys more comradeship with old friends, and, of course, nothing takes the place of either the Jaycee or the Jaycette movement when a young couple moves to another city or neighborhood. The Jaycette also gets leadership training, and is better equipped to work with organizations like the Parent-Teachers Association as a result.

Jaycettes can be of definite advantage to the local Junior Chambers, too. They can handle such things as phone calls and correspondence, and take over com-

pletely the projects that women do best, such as working with smaller children. Finally, and don't think it
hasn't been done, a would-be Jaycette must first get
her husband to the Junior Chamber.

The Wisconsin Jaycettes have compiled several pages
of possible activities—fund-raising projects, means of
increasing membership, program ideas, and hundreds
and hundreds of civic projects. If Wisconsin ever runs
out of civic projects, it will be a brave new world indeed.

Nor are all these projects limited to the state. When
a polio epidemic struck Rockford, Illinois, for example, Wisconsin Jaycettes dispatched four iron lungs to
the stricken town. A total of ninety-two children were
benefited by those lungs. Wisconsin Jaycettes also contributed $25,000 to the Cerebral Palsy Foundation.

One of the most active state Jaycette presidents was
Mrs. Bob Wimberley of Little Rock, Arkansas. During
Wanda's year of service, in 1955, she took it on herself
to make a complete survey of the Jaycette movement
in all the states. Writing as many as thirty-five letters
a day for days at a time, she tracked down auxiliaries
all over the United States, getting all the information
she could on their purposes, projects, organization,
membership drives, scrapbook rules, installation pro-
cedures, and ideas in general. She published a thousand
copies of the survey ("at no cost to anyone except the
Wimberleys") and sent them out to all state Jaycette
and Jaycee presidents. It was a terrific job, and in recognition of it, Wanda, surprised and tearful, was presented with a special award at the national convention
in Colorado Springs.

At the time of Wanda's survey Jaycettes were organized on a state level in eighteen states, and local auxiliaries existed in twenty more states and the District of Columbia. Many states and locals listed ambitious and successful projects. The Denton, Arkansas, Jaycettes, for example, presented the state mental hospital with three television sets. Results in the hospital were amazing. Patients who hadn't spoken a word for years all at once began to talk. Patients who could just lie on the floor began to get up to go to the recreation room to look at television. A real and permanent improvement took place in many places.

Wanda's survey revealed a wide divergence in qualifications for membership from city to city. In Haddonfield, New Jersey, a Jaycee's wife *or* sweetheart may be a Jaycette. In Albuquerque, New Mexico, the sister of a bachelor may belong. The good ladies of Huntington, Indiana, insist that the Jaycette be the wife of a Jaycee and a "woman of good character." Some locals require the Jaycette to drop out when her husband reaches the age of thirty-six; others require her to drop out when *she* reaches the age of thirty-six.

Jaycettes are proud of their rapid growth. The Georgia Jaycettes were organized at the state convention in Albany, 1955. The 1959 state president, Mrs. S. L. Broach, of Americus, was able to report that in four years they had increased membership to 1,100 Jaycettes in 58 chartered locals. They meet, incidentally, on Sunday morning, after having attended devotional services with their Jaycee husbands.

The Georgia Jaycettes even have their own creed, which ends:

"And we know so well the work that is done
   When husband and wife work together as one."

Gwen Broach, as a charter member of the Georgia Jaycettes, has visited all 58 clubs, most Jaycee regional meetings, state conventions, and national conventions. "I have made so many wonderful and lasting friendships in my immediate club, as well as throughout the state," she said. "What could be more rewarding!"

One of the most unlikely Jaycette presidents is Mrs. Billie Pitezel of the Tulsa Jaycee-ettes. Mrs. Pitezel, and her husband, Frank, a member of the Tulsa board of directors, have seven children.

"When our family first started growing," Mrs. Pitezel said, "I used them for an excuse for doing things. I didn't really need to stay home all the time, I was just lazy. But then I found myself getting bored."

Mrs. Pitezel is no longer bored. As Tulsa president she presides over a general meeting every second Monday night, executive board meeting once a month, supervises nine chairmen, frequently chipping in and doing committee work, too, and, finally, she is the Jaycee-ette delegate to luncheons of other organizations.

Why do these Jaycettes work so hard, accomplish so much? Here's the way Wanda Wimberley answered that, in her farewell speech as Arkansas president:

"Well, maybe it's the glow in a youngster's face when Santa visits him because of our efforts, or maybe it's the pride we feel in seeing a community development take shape, or perhaps it's a deep-seated feeling of personal satisfaction in giving a little unselfish service to other people and other things. Whatever it is, it is the dominating spark behind our efforts, yours and mine, as an auxiliary."

THE SOMETIME OF TOMORROW

IT'S SATURDAY MORNING in St. Louis, and the big, new, shiny building of the Community Federal Savings and Loan Association is closed for the weekend, offices and corridors hushed and still. But the building is not completely deserted. There's a light in the office of the president. In this large, tastefully decorated room the building's lone occupant, a stocky man who walks with a springy stride and wears an eager smile, shuffles through a folder on his desk, then swivels around to face a strange-looking antique of a typewriter.

They are old friends, these two; they understand each other. The olive-green Oliver typewriter is in its forties, the man in his sixties. The typewriter shows signs of age—the dark-green enamel has worn off in places, leaving shiny metal—but it still works perfectly, even though it has never been oiled or repaired. The man, too, shows evidence of the years, in the smile-crinkled corners of eyes and mouth, but he is also healthy and hearty and, today of all days, happy as well.

For he is John H. Armbruster, one of the early members of the Junior Chamber of Commerce, and the Keeper of *The Log of the S.S. Fellowship*. Nearly every Saturday and Sunday of his life, for over a quarter of a century, John has come down to the office to type out the log, all alone. For to him, this is a labor of love. And to every Jaycee, past, present, and future, this labor has meaning. For it carries on the Jaycee fellowship.

When John's term as national director of the Junior Chamber expired in 1931, he felt a tinge of sadness at the thought that many of his Jaycee friendships might wither on the vine. He resolved to do something to keep those friendships alive, and the log was the result. Restricted to past national officers and directors of the Junior Chamber, the crew has steadily increased over the years to where it numbers over 650 members.

Over the years, too, John Armbruster's fortunes have also increased. He organized this Savings and Loan Association, first in the St. Louis area, in a meeting hall above a tavern. He couldn't afford to pay rent but surely, he told the cafe owner, some of the people who came would buy refreshments later. Today Community Federal has a paid-up capital of over $450,000.

As he built his business and devoted weekends to his log, John was also active in the International Young Men's Christian Association and Rotary International. When he was asked to head up the St. Louis fund raising committee for YMCA Buildings for Brotherhood, all over the world, he wrote to fellow Jaycees and Rotarians in all the communities these buildings were planned, asking if they were really necessary, if the local people were doing their share. Letters came back from every community—towns in Japan, Korea, Formosa, Hong Kong, Pakistan, India, Israel, and in other countries in Asia, Africa, and Europe—assuring him that the project was indeed worthwhile. Then John Armbruster went to work, and under his direction St.

Louis oversubscribed its quota before any other community came close.

John also wrote *The First Twenty-five Years of the Junior Chamber of Commerce*, the organization's first history. But it is as Keeper of the Log that he is best known. The log is a clearing house of information for all its crew. Who made a million, who was elected governor, who took a trip around the world. Every issue contains proof of Jaycee brotherhood. As for example the time the ministerial board of an Episcopal church in Florida, looking for a new minister, heard of a likely prospect in a town in northern Iowa. But how could they be sure he was the right man? One of the board members was a Jaycee. He met a Jaycee from western Iowa vacationing in the town, and told him the problem. The Jaycee from western Iowa promptly called a Jaycee in Des Moines, who contacted a Jaycee in the minister's home town. Back down the line went a glowing report. And the Episcopal Church got a new minister, thanks to three Jaycees—whose religions, incidentally, happened to be Jewish, Catholic, and Lutheran, respectively.

John gets his reward for his warm and wonderful labor of love in every mail. After meeting with a group in Lincoln, Nebraska, one Sunday morning, he received a letter from one of them, Francis J. Minard, saying:

"Thanks, again, John, for giving us your time last Sunday. In his pastoral letter that morning our minister prayed for God's help to align ourselves with forces that promote good and deter evil. And I thanked God for the S.S. Fellowship and its crew."

Twenty years after starting the log, in 1951, John

attended the dedication ceremonies of the War Memorial in Tulsa. On the plane coming back with him was Philip T. R. Pugsley, past president of the Canada Junior Chamber and then president of Junior Chamber International.

"John," Pugsley said, "your work with the crew is so wonderful, don't you think you could make it world-wide, to take in all our JCI senators?"

And so *The Elder Statesman* was born. It too is a clearing house of information, only on an international level. When a senator plans a trip—and some travel constantly—he always sends John his itinerary for inclusion in *The Elder Statesman*. Frequently he'll check into a hotel 10,000 miles from home to find messages from other Senators waiting for him.

Truly the Jaycee movement is bringing the peoples of the world closer together, day after day. *The Elder Statesman* reports case after case of international friendship, based entirely on what its readers write John Armbruster. On one occasion John was even able to report a case of good fellowship breaking through the Iron Curtain. It happened in Edinburgh, where the Jaycees gave a special luncheon for Russian Ambassador Malik and his wife, presented Mrs. Malik with a hand-made Tartan doll, then took the two for a sight-seeing trip around the city.

Although many of the letters which pour into John's office from all over the world contain specific information, many, on the other hand, simply thank him for his service to the brotherhood of mankind.

"The world is hungry for friendship," a typical letter will read, "and this is what you bring us."

And around Christmas time the mail is particularly heartwarming, for then the Christmas cards come in. Delicate pastels from Portugal, bright gay cards from Iceland, big, handsome cards from Israel, small cards with drawings of appealing, moon-faced, dark-skinned children from Mexico and Central America.

"These," John Armbruster says, holding up a handful, "are the dividends of my work. But the basic purpose of the log is to provide a means by which the close fellowship of all Jaycees, of yesterday, today and tomorrow, will never die, but will go on and on into the future."

Another Jaycee with continuing dividends is C. J. McConville of Minneapolis. In connection with the thirteenth JCI World Congress, held in Minneapolis, Mac dreamed up the national project, "Host to the World," sold it, and became national chairman. By arranging for Junior Chambers throughout the United States to be hosts to JCI delegates from all over the world, Mac made it possible for the delegates both to meet Americans in their homes, and to save money and thereby stay in America longer.

The program involved a fantastic amount of paper work. Mac arranged, by mail, itineraries of over 700 individuals and groups all across the country. This meant constant correspondence, with many carbons and in many languages between Mac and the traveler and Mac and the Jaycee hosts in every city in order to pin down all the details. An Australian contingent of eighty delegates chartered a bus and traveled from San Francisco to Minneapolis and back to Los Angeles through New York and Miami, stopping for coffee breaks, lunch, and dinner en route, and being put up overnight by Jaycees in whatever city they landed. Every stop was prearranged.

Out of such get-togethers grew lasting friendships, correspondence, and even international visits, cutting across boundary lines, bringing the Jaycees of the world even closer in brotherhood and understanding.

In Hartford, Wisconsin, population 5,000, when George J. Bruns suggested inviting some foreign delegates to Hartford even his fellow Jaycees thought he was out of his head. "Why would anybody want to come halfway around the world to visit a small town like Hartford?" they asked.

But Bruns was persistent. Even McConville, who also felt that delegates would prefer to visit big cities, finally broke down and sent him a list of delegates coming from France, South Africa, and Algeria. Bruns got out the letters of invitation—and back came more acceptances than the town could possibly handle. Algeria, for one, wanted to bring all twenty-eight delegates to Hartford.

Finally, after much more correspondence, Bruns got it all straightened out. The Hartford Jaycees were hosts to five delegates from France, including their past national president, and JCI vice-president for Europe, Yvon Choutard; seven from Algeria, and three from South Africa. The hosts took them through local industries, to their monthly meeting, to luncheon meetings of Rotary and Lions clubs, and to their homes. And this was all just exactly what the visitors wanted to see.

All the time the delegates were there the farmers'

apple show was going on. Basil Rochfort, of Durban, leader of the South African contingent, literally ate that up; he sampled every apple and every apple pie. With audacity, aplomb, English accent, and charm, he sold the isolationist Wisconsin farmers on internationalism, right then and there. He also provided a bit of news to a local reporter covering the event, who reported that "Basil Rochfort, from South Africa, spoke in perfect English."

Since the visitation, things have not been the same in Hartford. The local paper, whose publisher hosted a charming French couple, has not been so outstandingly isolationist. Members of the Lions, Rotary, and Senior Chamber still talk about what fine fellows those foreign Jaycees were. And George Bruns, who started the whole thing purely as something different, has become much in demand as a speaker throughout the state.

And perhaps more important than anything else is the flood of mail, including tape recordings and movies, that now goes back and forth between Hartford and South Africa, France, and Algeria. In just two families, the Brunses and the Rochforts, correspondence goes on in two media—letters and tapes—and on three levels —George and Basil, George's wife and Basil's wife, and George's daughter and Basil's son (both eleven years old).

Many people in Hartford—not just Jaycees—now correspond regularly with their new friends abroad. From this warm kernel of international friendship, who knows what will grow?

Is it too wild a dream to hope that from such friendships will come world understanding and unity? Or, as Henry Giessenbier once hoped, "that a message will come in the sometime of tomorrow that will stir the people toward the establishment of a permanent and everlasting world peace?"

At least one Jaycee doesn't think so. He is Maurice Sexton, JCI president. After traveling over half the world, seeing first hand the great changes the Jaycee young men have already wrought, Maurice returned home to Palmerston North to get a breath before resuming. One afternoon his ten-year-old son was looking for something to do. Maurice took a JCI world map, showing where Junior Chambers were located, and cut it into pieces.

"Here," he said to the boy, "see if you can put it back together again."

In a matter of seconds, there it was, all complete. Maurice was amazed. "How did you do that so quickly?" he asked.

The boy smiled, turned it over. On the reverse was the Jaycee Emblem. "Everybody knows what the Jaycee emblem looks like, Dad," he said. "I just put the Jaycee emblem back together and that way I put the world back together."

Maurice looked at the map of the world, now all in one piece, at the smiling boy, a Jaycee of the future.

"How right you are!" he breathed. "That emblem represents the brotherhood of mankind, the finest in humanity. It represents people from all over the world, from different lands, speaking different tongues, but all working together. Yes, it's true—through the Jaycee emblem we can unite the world!"

ABOUT THE AUTHOR

Mr. Herndon was born and raised in Charlottesville, Virginia, and being the true Virginian that he is, returned there eight years ago with his wife and children to pursue his career as a free-lance writer. After attending the University of Missouri and the University of Virginia, he worked for New Orleans newspapers for several years. With the U.S. Army during World War II, he participated in the Normandy invasion and four other major European campaigns. After his military duty, he went to New York to get started on a serious writing career. A well-known magazine writer, Mr. Herndon has written articles for many of the major magazines throughout the country and is also the author of *Bergdorf's on the Plaza*.